TWENTIETH CENTURY ONE ACT PLAYS

Contrasts in Drama

selected and edited by

JOSEPH SHERMAN MA, LTCL

Senior English Master
King Edward VII School
Johannesburg

Edward Arnold

© Joseph Sherman 1975

First published in Great Britain 1975
by Edward Arnold (Publishers) Ltd.,
25 Hill Street, London W1X 8LL

ISBN: 0 7131 1925 X

Set in 10 on 11½ pt Photon Baskerville and printed in Great Britain by
The Camelot Press Ltd, Southampton

Contents

Acknowledgments

The Publisher's thanks are due to the following for permission to reproduce copyright material:

Calder and Boyars Ltd for Arrabal's 'The Two Executioners', trans. Barbara Wright (Margaret Ramsey Ltd, London); Mr Eric Bentley, New York, for his English translation of Anton Chekhov's 'A Wedding'; the Pirandello Administration. The International Copyright Bureau Ltd and Mr Eric Bentley for the English translation of Pirandello's 'The Man with a Flower in his Mouth'; Macmillan and Co. Ltd and Mrs E. O'Casey for Sean O'Casey's 'The End of the Beginning' from *Collected Plays*, Vol. I and *Five One-Act Plays*; Eyre Methuen Ltd for Harold Pinter's 'The Room'; Editions Gallimard, Paris and Hamish Hamilton Ltd for Jean-Paul Sartre's 'The Trojan Women', trans. Ronald Duncan © 1967, and 'This Property is Condemned' from *27 Wagons Full of Cotton* © 1945 by Tennessee Williams, © 1953 by Tennessee Williams.

PERFORMING RIGHTS
Permission to perform the plays in this anthology should be obtained from the copyright holders, except in the case of *The Trojan Women* for which application should be made to Eric Glass Ltd, 28 Berkeley Square, London W1.

Introduction

The one-act play has long been established as a dramatic form of great significance. More and more of today's best dramatists are turning to it because they have realised that in the theatre it does not take a ton of dynamite to make a great explosion.

This anthology contrasts seven one-act plays with one another to show the wide range and impact of the one-act play. Every play in this anthology was written with a serious purpose and demands serious attention. Moreover, each play is in its own way a theatrical *tour de force*, providing the widest possible scope for the talents of the actor, director and designer alike, and in good presentations, demanding the complete involvement of audiences on every level.

Too often, people in a theatre lose sight of the purpose behind what they are doing or seeing: they fail to see the mainspring of the work of art, and fail to relate it to their own lives and experiences. Works of art do not exist in isolation, admired and valued for themselves alone, without reference to the world in which they appear or the people to whom they speak. Nor do they exist solely to entertain. The entertainment which they provide is not their end, but the means they use to serve a more significant end. Art derives from the artist's concern with the world around him and its influence upon him; it is a vision of that world which has revealed itself to him, and which he wishes to communicate to us. There are as many visions as there are men; as many means of communicating them as there are skills. Yet since they all have the same basic motivation, they hope at bottom to achieve the same end. This is what gives works of art at the same time their uniqueness and their universality.

Of all kinds of art, perhaps none is more immediate in its communication with all kinds of people than the theatre. A play speaks with a directness, a clarity and an ease denied to other art forms. The seven diverse one-act plays brought together in this anthology contrast with one another on almost every possible level—in the attitude they adopt towards life; in the characters they create to present this attitude; in the theatrical devices they employ to give this attitude dramatic expression; in the effect they are meant to have on those who read or watch them. Yet fundamentally they are all doing the same thing—they are revealing and communicating something about life, something which develops or increases our awareness and understanding of it; forces us to reconsider principles and premises to which we may be clinging even though they are outworn; compels us to see people and their problems in a way we could not do unaided. In the very contrast and conflict of ideas presented lies the hope that ultimately we may be able to revaluate ourselves and our environment in terms that will make them more truly important to us.

The theatre has always been the place where new ideas, and the new forms which must be devised to present them if they are to have the most powerful impact, have received their most exciting expression. Here ideas leave the undemanding passivity of the printed page, and become translated into vividly dramagic action. We may ignore the challenge of the printed word by shutting the book; it is not so easy to escape the challenge of a dramatic performance that demands both the attention and the participation of the spectators.

Several of the plays in this anthology have angered and upset spectators in the past: it is to be hoped that they will long continue to do so. As long as they challenge, disturb or move those who watch them, so long shall we have both a meaningful theatre and a thinking society. Complacency is too often the vice of theatre-goers. They too soon grow accustomed to expecting all plays to fit the same pattern, to offer them the same things. Fortunately for the theatre, most serious playwrights refuse to be so stereotyped. Each one insists on operating in his own independent manner, on presenting truth in his own unique way. Hence the title of this anthology. The contrasts provided by the plays in it show the impossibility of complacency in the living theatre. They also show the remarkable powers of that theatre. Just as the ideas they present are often startling, even shocking, so is the manner of their presentation.

So this anthology has a double aim. It offers plays serious enough in content to be read and studied, and plays exciting and challenging enough to be produced. A play is only fully alive when it is performed and watched, and demanding as is much of the material offered here for both actor and spectator, its rewards are concomitantly greater for both. Never bound by any conventional fetters of form, the one-act play has continually swept them aside and become a vehicle for the most *avant garde*, revolutionary developments in the theatre—indeed, it has become in itself the revolution, breaking down conventions of time and space; destroying old notions of what constituted 'the well-made play'; leaving audiences constantly dazed, stunned or satisfied. Those who would know what is happening in today's theatre must know its one-act plays. It is hoped that the contrasts of this anthology will whet many appetites for more of that knowledge.

Although I have offered some information about the play wrights, and have raised some points for consideration about each play to stimulate discussion, readers and producers will obviously find their own particular points of contrast. The more they find, the better will the aim of this anthology be served. If it raises questions and provokes thought about the purposes and directions of our lives, and challenges the intellectual and creative energies of reader, producer and spectator, it will more than have achieved it purpose.

Joseph Sherman

CHEKHOV

A Wedding

The reputation of Anton Chekhov (1860–1904) as the foremost exponent of naturalistic drama rests mainly on his four major plays, *The Seagull, Uncle Vanya, Three Sisters* and *The Cherry Orchard.* About the purpose of drama, Chekhov maintained:

> 'A play ought to be written in which the people should come and go, dine, talk of the weather, or play cards, not because the author wants it, but because that is what happens in real life. . . . It is necessary that on the stage everything should be as complex and as simple as in life. People are having dinner, and while they are having it, their future happiness may be decided, or their lives may be about to be shattered.'

Yet coupled to his avowed desire to depict life as it really is, is a desperate longing to see life as it could and should be, and to impart a powerful sense of this vision to others. In a letter to a friend in 1902, Chekhov explained:

> 'You tell me that people cry at my plays. I've heard others say the same. But that was not why I wrote them. . . . All I wanted was to say honestly to people: "Have a look at yourselves and see how bad and dreary your lives are!" The important thing is that people should realise that, for when they do, they will most certainly create another and better life for themselves. I will not live to see it, but I know that it will be quite different, quite unlike our present life. And so long as this different life does not exist, I shall go on saying to people again and again, "Please, understand that your life is bad and dreary!" What is there in this to cry about?'

Such a wish seems almost naïve, for seventy years after Chekhov's death, human life appears just as bad and dreary as ever—perhaps more so. But Chekhov is not an unrealistic idealist. While his plays never cease to invoke visions of an ideal happiness in a perfect world, these are continually undercut by the harsh facts of a reality which negates such visions. Essentially Chekhov perceives that man is the prisoner of his own limitations both of action and aspiration, and however much he may dream, what he does, or fails to do, takes him further and further away from ever realising those dreams. Indeed, those dreams themselves appear to be desperate means of escape from a world whose triviality and apparent futility become stifling and unbearable. However desperate the plight of Chekhov's characters may seem at any given moment, their naïve escapism and inability to act positively diminish their tragic status by making them absurd.

In perceiving this, Chekhov is truly able to see life as it is: not as unremitting tragedy occasionally relieved by humour, but as a complex balance of tragedy and triviality, of agony and absurdity. His plays, as dramatic expressions of such a vision, are not sombre expositions to which comic or farcical elements have been superadded; they represent a kind of drama in which tragic and comic elements merge to express more accurately the true nature of life itself.

Perhaps this purpose is most immediately apparent in Chekhov's one-act farces, which are a highly complex blend of satirical and psychological detail with elements of traditional farce, so that they tend to present a view of a world not only 'bad and dreary' but mad, disorientated and destructive. In this they anticipate the work of the later Absurdists, but they are redeemed from the utter despair of those by the two qualities of humour and love which inform all of Chekhov's writing. His hope for 'another and better life', so conspicuously absent from the work of Beckett, Pinter and Arrabal, is what ultimately gives his one-act plays their gaiety and incentive for change.

A Wedding, drawn from Chekhov's rich personal observation and experience at a time when he lived below an apartment rented out for weddings, throws into farcical relief the contemporary custom among Moscow lower middle classes of hiring high-ranking officers or civil servants to lend lustre to their wedding receptions. Adapted from two of his own short stories, *A Marriage of Convenience* and *A Wedding with a General*, the play is a perfect illustration of the way good farce is created, and an object lesson to those who believe that farce cannot make a serious and pertinent comment about the human condition.

CHARACTERS

ZIGALOV, *the bride's father*
MRS ZIGALOV, *the bride's mother*
THE BRIDE
APLOMBOV, *the bridegroom*
THE BEST MAN
YAT, *a telegraph clerk*
MRS ZMEYUKIN, *a midwife*
DIMBA, *a Greek confectioner*
NYUNIN, *an insurance clerk*
'GENERAL' REVUNOV
A SAILOR
A WAITER

A Wedding

The scene is a private room in a second-rate restaurant. Brilliantly lit. Large table laid for supper. WAITERS *in tails busy at this and other tables. Behind the scenes, a band playing the last figure of a quadrille. Three figures cross the stage:* MRS ZMEYUKIN, *a midwife;* YAT, *a telegraph clerk; and the* BEST MAN. *The* MIDWIFE *is crying 'No, no, no!'*

TELEGRAPH CLERK: [*On her heels*]   Have pity on me! [*But she keeps on crying 'No, no, no!'*]

BEST MAN: [*Following*]   Now look, you can't carry on like that! Where are you going? What about the *Grand Rond? Grand Rond, s'il vous plaît!*

[*All three are off stage*]

[*Enter* APLOMBOV, *the bridegroom and* MRS ZIGALOV, *the bride's mother*]

BRIDE'S MOTHER: Now, instead of bothering me with all this talk, why don't you just go and dance?

BRIDEGROOM: I can't make figure eights with my feet, I'm no Spinoza, I'm a practical man, a man of character, I find nothing amusing in idle pursuits. But dancing is not the point. Forgive me, mother dear, but there's a great deal in your conduct that I can't figure out. For example, quite apart from furniture, utensils, miscellaneous effects, you promised to give me, with your daughter, two lottery tickets. Where are they?

BRIDE'S MOTHER: My poor head, it's aching again, it must be the weather, they say it's going to thaw.

BRIDEGROOM: Don't try to wriggle out of it. You pawned those tickets. I found out only this afternoon. You're an exploiter, mother dear. Excuse the expression, but you are. I speak without prejudice. I don't want the confounded tickets. It's a matter of principle. And I don't like being gypped. I am making your daughter the happiest of women and if you don't get those tickets back I'll make mincemeat of her into the bargain. I'm a man of honour, don't forget.

BRIDE'S MOTHER: [*Counting the places at table*]   One, two, three, four, five . . .

A WAITER: The cook says how would you like the ice cream, ma'am?

BRIDE'S MOTHER: How do you mean: how would I like the ice cream?

WAITER: With rum, with Madeira, or with nothing, ma'am?

BRIDEGROOM: With rum, you fool. And tell the head waiter there isn't enough wine. We need some Haut Sauterne as well. [*To* BRIDE'S MOTHER]   There was another agreement: you promised me a general. You swore to deliver a general as a wedding guest. Where is he?

BRIDE'S MOTHER: It's not my fault, my dear.

BRIDEGROOM: Whose fault is it, for heaven's sake?

BRIDE'S MOTHER: Nyunin's. The insurance man. He was here yesterday, he swore he'd dig up a general, but I suppose he just couldn't find one. We're as sorry as you are. There's nothing we wouldn't do for you. When *you* say a general, a general it should be . . .

BRIDEGROOM: Another thing. Everyone knows that telegraph clerk courted Dashenka before me. Why must you invite him to our wedding? Have you no consideration for my feelings?

BRIDE'S MOTHER: Well, er . . . what's your name again? Yes: Aplombov. My dear Aplombov, you have been married just two hours, and already you have us both worn out—me and my daughter—with your incessant talk, talk, talk. How will it be a year from now? Think of *that*.

BRIDEGROOM: So you don't like to hear the truth. I see. But that's no excuse for having no sense of honour. I want you to have a sense of honour!

[*Couples cross the stage, dancing the Grand Rond. The first couple are the* BRIDE *and the* BEST MAN. *The* MIDWIFE *and the* TELEGRAPH CLERK *come last and stay behind, Enter* ZIGALOV, *the bride's father and* DIMBA, *a Greek confectioner. During the cross and afterwards in the wings, the* BEST MAN *is shouting: 'Promenade! Promenade Messieurs-dames! Promenade!'*]

TELEGRAPH CLERK: [*To the* MIDWIFE]   Have pity on me, enchanting one!

MIDWIFE: Listen to him . . . My dear fellow, I've told you: I am not in good voice today!

TELEGRAPH CLERK: Just a couple of notes! One! One note! Have pity on me!

MIDWIFE: You bother me. [*She sits down and vigorously uses her fan*]

TELEGRAPH CLERK: But you have no pity. A monster of cruelty, if I may so express myself, with the voice of a goddess! You've no right being a midwife with a voice like that. You should be a concert singer. Your rendering of that phrase—how does it go?—yes, um: [*He sings*]

> I loved you though 'twas all in vain!

Exquisite!

MIDWIFE: [*Singing*]

> I loved you—and may do again!

Is that the bit you mean?

TELEGRAPH CLERK: That's it. Exquisite!

MIDWIFE: But I am not in voice today. Fan me. It's hot. [*To* BRIDEGROOM] Why are you so sad, Aplombov? On your wedding day? What are you thinking of?

BRIDEGROOM: It's a serious step—marriage. Must be given serious thought—from every angle.

MIDWIFE: What sceptics you all are! Unbelievers! I can't breathe among you. Give me air! Air! [*She practises a few notes of song*]

TELEGRAPH CLERK: Exquisite!

MIDWIFE: Fan me! My heart's about to burst! Answer me one question: *why* am I suffocating?

TELEGRAPH CLERK: You've been sweating such a lot—

MIDWIFE: Such a word in my presence!

TELEGRAPH CLERK: Many apologies. I was forgetting you move in aristocratic circles, if I may so express myself.

MIDWIFE: Oh, stop it. Give me poetry! Heavenly raptures! And fan me, fan me.

BRIDE'S FATHER: [*In tipsy conversation with the* GREEK] Another? [*Fills his glass*] Every time is the right time for a drink. As long as your work gets done, eh, Dimba? Drink and . . . drink and . . . drink again [*They drink*] Do you have tigers—in Greece?

THE GREEK: [*Showing the whites of his eyes*] I'll say!

BRIDE'S FATHER: And lions?

GREEK: Lions, tigers, everything! In Russia—nothing. In Greece—everything. That's the whole difference between Russia and Greece.

BRIDE'S FATHER: Everything?

GREEK: Everything: my father, my uncle, all my brothers . . .

BRIDE'S FATHER: You have whales too—in Greece?

GREEK: Everything. Whales, sharks . . .

BRIDE'S MOTHER: [*To her husband*] Time to sit down, my dear. And hands off the canned lobster—it's for the General—I still think there'll be a General—

BRIDE'S FATHER: You have lobsters—in Greece?

GREEK: Everything! Everything I tell you—

BRIDE'S FATHER: Civil servants too?

MIDWIFE: The air must be divine—in Greece.

BRIDE'S FATHER: Have another.

BRIDE'S MOTHER: No time for another! It's past eleven. Time to sit down!

BRIDE'S FATHER: Sit down? Good idea! Sit down! Sit down, everyone!

[*And his wife joins him in calling to all the guests, on stage and off, to take their places at table*]

MIDWIFE: [*Sitting*]   Give me poetry!

        His quest for storms will never cease
        For only storms can bring him peace!

Give me storms!

TELEGRAPH CLERK: [*Aside*]   Isn't she remarkable? I'm head over heels in love with her.

[*Enter the* BRIDE, *a* SAILOR, *the* BEST MAN, *other wedding guests. They sit down noisily. Pause. The band plays a march*]

THE SAILOR: [*Rising*]   Ladies and gentlemen, as we have a great many toasts and speeches ahead of us, I propose we start at once—with the greatest toast of them all. I give you: the bride and groom!

[ALL *cry: 'The bride and groom' and clink glasses and drink. The band plays a flourish*]

SAILOR: And now: it needs sweetening!

ALL: It needs sweetening.

[*The* BRIDE *and* GROOM *kiss*]

TELEGRAPH CLERK: Exquisite! Ladies and gentlemen: credit where credit is due! Let us give thanks for a splendid party in a splendid setting! What a magnificent establishment this is! Only one thing lacking: electric light—if I may so express myself. They have it all over the world. Everywhere but Mother Russia. [*He sits, sadly*]

BRIDE'S FATHER: Yes, um, electric light. Come to think of it, electric light is a hoax. They slip a piece of coal in when no one's looking. So, my good man, if you want to give us light, give us good old-fashioned light, none of these superintellectual notions.

TELEGRAPH CLERK: Take a look at a battery some time. That's no superintellectual notion.

BRIDE'S FATHER: Certainly not! I've no wish to be caught looking at such a thing. [*Severely*] And I'm sorry to find you sympathising with tricksters and swindlers, young man, when you should be having a drink and handing the bottle round!

BRIDEGROOM: I quite agree, father dear. Not that I object to scientific discoveries on principle. But there's a time for everything. [*To his bride*]   What do you say, *ma chère?*

BRIDE: Some people like to show off and talk so no one can understand a word.

BRIDE'S MOTHER: Don't worry, my dear, your father and I never got mixed up in this education business, not in all our lives. And you're the third daughter we've found a good Russian husband for. [*To* TELEGRAPH CLERK] Why do you have to come here if you think we're so uneducated? Why not go to your educated friends?

TELEGRAPH CLERK: I respect you and your family very much, Mrs Zigalov. I wasn't trying to show off, mentioning electric light. I've always wished Dashenka would find a good husband. And it isn't easy these days, with everyone marrying for money . . .

BRIDEGROOM: A dig at me.

TELEGRAPH CLERK: [*Scared*] That's not true! That was a . . . general observation . . . present company always excepted, if I may so express myself. Heavens, everyone knows *you're* marrying for love. The dowry isn't worth talking about.

BRIDE'S MOTHER. What? Not worth talking about, isn't it? You'd better watch your tongue. A thousand rubles in cash, three fur coats, complete furniture and linen. Try and find a dowry to match that!

TELEGRAPH CLERK: But I didn't mean . . . The furniture's splendid of course . . . I wasn't getting in any digs!

BRIDE'S MOTHER: Well, don't. We invited you on your parents' account, so don't go sticking *your* oar in. If you knew Aplombov was marrying her for money, why couldn't you have said so before? [*Tearfully*] I nursed her, I raised her, if she'd been a diamond I couldn't have treasured her more, my child, my emerald . . .

BRIDEGROOM: So you believe him! Thank you so much, thank you *so* much! [*To* TELEGRAPH CLERK] As for you, Mr Yat, friend of the family as you are, I cannot permit you to carry on like this in other folks' houses. Kindly take yourself off.

TELEGRAPH CLERK: How do you mean?

BRIDEGROOM: What a pity you're not a real gentleman—like myself! That being so, however, take yourself off.

[*The band plays a flourish*]

VARIOUS GENTLEMEN: [*To* BRIDEGROOM] Come off it, Aplombov, old boy! Leave him alone, old man. Don't spoil the fun. Take your seat. [*Etc.*]

TELEGRAPH CLERK: But I never . . . why, I . . . I honestly don't understand . . . Certainly, I'll go . . . But first give me the five rubles you borrowed a year ago to buy yourself a *piqué* waistcoat, if I may so express myself. Then I'll have one more drink and, um, go. But first give me the money.

THE GENTLEMEN: Take your seats. Drop it now. Much ado about nothing. [*Etc.*]

BEST MAN: [*Shouting*]   To the bride's parents, Mr and Mrs Zigalov! [*The cry is taken up by the others who clink and drink. The band plays a flourish*]

ZIGALOV: [*Touched, bowing in all directions*]   Thank you, my friends, thank you for not forgetting us, for not snubbing us. I don't put it this way from false modesty, I have no ulterior motive, I'm not planning to cheat you in any way, I speak as I feel, in the simplicity of my heart, I begrudge you nothing, you are my friends, and I . . . I thank you!

[*He kisses those near him*]

BRIDE: [*To her mother*]   Mama, you're crying! Why is that? I'm so happy!

BRIDEGROOM: Your mother's upset at the approaching separation from you. But I wouldn't advise her to forget our little talk.

TELEGRAPH CLERK: Don't cry, Mrs Zigalov! What *are* tears, scientifically speaking? Nothing but neurotic weakness!

BRIDE'S FATHER: You have mushrooms—in Greece?

GREEK: Everything. We have everything.

BRIDE'S FATHER: Bet you don't have brown mushrooms. Like ours.

GREEK: Every kind! Every kind!

BRIDE'S FATHER: All right, Dimba, old man, now it's your turn to make a speech. Ladies and gentlemen, Mr Dimba is going to make a speech!

ALL: A speech! Mr Dimba! Come on, Dimba! [*Etc.*]

GREEK: But why? What for? I don't see it!

MIDWIFE: It's your turn! Make it snappy!

GREEK: [*Stands, confused*]   All I can say is . . . There's Russia . . . and there's Greece . . . In Russia, there are many people . . . In Greece . . . there are many people . . . On the sea, there are ships . . . In Russia, that is . . . On land, railways . . . You are Russians, we are Greeks, I want nothing for myself. There's Russia, and there's Greece . . .

[*Enter* NYUNIN, *the aforementioned insurance man*]

INSURANCE MAN: One moment, ladies and gentlemen, just one moment! Mrs Zigalov, may I have your attention? [*He takes her on one side*]   You shall have your general. He's on his way over. A real live general aged eighty. Or maybe ninety.

BRIDE'S MOTHER: When will he get here?

INSURANCE MAN: Any minute. You'll be grateful to me till your dying day.

BRIDE'S MOTHER: A real general.

INSURANCE MAN: Well, almost real. Actually, he was in the navy. They called him Captain. That's naval lingo for General.

BRIDE'S MOTHER: You couldn't be deceiving me, could you?

INSURANCE MAN: Am I a swindler?

BRIDE'S MOTHER: Oh, no!

INSURANCE MAN: Thank you.

BRIDE'S MOTHER: It's just that I don't like to spend money for nothing.

INSURANCE MAN: Rest easy. He's a model general. [*Raising his voice for all to hear*] 'General,' I said, 'general, you've been forgetting us lately!' [*Sits down at table among the guests*] ''Pon my soul, Nyunin, my boy,' said the general to me, 'how can I go to a wedding when I don't even know the bridegroom?' 'What's wrong with the bridegroom?' I rejoined. 'Splendid, open-hearted fellow that he is!' 'What does he do?' says the general. 'Do?' says I, 'do? Why he's the valuer in a pawnshop.' 'Oh!' says the general. 'Oh what?' says I, 'the best of men work in pawn-shops these days, also the best of women.' At this he clapped me on the shoulder, we smoked a Havana together, and . . .

BRIDEGROOM: When will he get here?

INSURANCE MAN: Any minute. He was putting his rubbers on when I left.

BRIDEGROOM: We must have them play a military march.

INSURANCE MAN: Bandmaster! *Marche militaire!*

A WAITER: General Revunov!

[*As the band strikes up with a march,* 'GENERAL' REVUNOV *enters.* NYUNIN *and both* ZIGALOVS *rush to greet him*]

BRIDE'S MOTHER: General Revunov, welcome to our home!

'GENERAL': Delighted I'm sure.

BRIDE'S FATHER: We aren't celebrities, General, we aren't millionaires, but don't think the worse of us on that account. We won't cheat you. We begrudge you nothing. You are welcome.

'GENERAL': Delighted I'm sure.

INSURANCE MAN: General Revunov, allow me to present the bridegroom, Mr Aplombov, along with his newly born, I mean newly married, bride, the former Miss Zigalov. Mr Yat of the Telegraph Office. Mr Dimba, noted confectioner of Greek descent . . . And so forth. The rest aren't worth much. Why don't you sit down, General?

'GENERAL': Delighted I'm sure. [*But he doesn't sit down. He takes* NYUNIN *on one side*] One moment, ladies and gentlemen, a confidential conference! [*Whispering*] What do you mean:

General? There are no generals in the navy! I was captain of the smallest ship in the fleet. The rank is equivalent to colonel!

INSURANCE MAN: [*Speaking over-distinctly into his ear as to a deaf man*] Let us call you General. It's simpler. These folks respect their betters. Resign yourself to being their betters!

'GENERAL': Oh. Oh, I see. [*Goes meekly back to table*] Delighted I'm sure.

BRIDE'S MOTHER: Take a seat, General. We can't give you the dainty food you're used to, but if our simple fare should take your fancy . . .

'GENERAL': [*Not following this*] What? What's that? Oh, yes. [*Long silence*] I live plainly, ma'am. Everyone lived plainly in the old days. [*Another silence*] When Nyunin invited me here, I said to him: 'That could be awkward, I don't know them.' 'What of it?' said Nyunin. 'These folk respect their betters!' 'They do?' I replied, 'well, that's different. And it's awfully boring at home.'

BRIDE'S FATHER: So you came out of pure generosity, General. How much I respect that! We're plain folks. We won't cheat you. Have something to eat, General.

BRIDEGROOM: Have you been out of the service long, General?

'GENERAL': What? Oh, yes. Very true. Yes. But what's this? This herring is bitter. This bread is bitter . . .

ALL: It needs sweetening!

[BRIDE *and* GROOM *kiss*]

'GENERAL': [*Chuckling*] Your health, your health! [*Silence*] In the old days, everything was plain. I like that. Of course, I'm getting on. Seventy-two. Retired from the service in sixty-five. [*Silence*] On occasion, of course, they used to make a bit of a splash—in the old days . . . [*His eye lights on the sailor*] Aren't you a sailor?

SAILOR: Yes, sir.

'GENERAL': [*Relaxing considerably*] Ah! Yes. The navy. Not an easy life. Always something to think about. Every word has a special meaning. 'Top-sheets and main-sail, mast-hands aloft!' Isn't that good? And what does it mean? Your sailor knows! He, he, he!

INSURANCE MAN: To General Revunov!

[*The band plays a flourish. All cheer*]

TELEGRAPH CLERK: Thanks for telling us about the problems of the navy, General. But what about the telegraph service? You can't go in for modern telegraphy without French and German. Transmitting telegrams is no easy matter. Listen.

[*He taps out code with his fork on the table*]

'GENERAL': What does it mean?

TELEGRAPH CLERK: It means: 'Oh, how I respect all your noble qualities, General!' D'you think that's easy? Now.

[*He taps again*]

'GENERAL': Louder. I can't hear.

TELEGRAPH CLERK: [*Loudly*]   'How happy am I, dear madam, to hold you in my arms!'

'GENERAL': What madam is that? Oh. Oh yes. [*Turning to the* SAILOR]   In the face of a hundred-mile-an-hour headwind, always hoist your foretop halyards, my boy and your topsail halyards too! When the sails get loose, take hold of the foresail and foretopsail halyards and the topgallant braces . . .

INSURANCE MAN: Our guests are bored, Revunov, they don't understand.

'GENERAL': I'll explain. If the ship is lying with the wind on the starboard tack under full sail, and you want to bring her round before the wind, pipe all hands on deck, and as soon as they've run up, give the command: 'To your places! Round before the wind!' The men pull the stays and braces and, oh, what a life it is, in spite of yourself you leap up and shout: 'Bravo! Bravo, brave lads!'

[*He breaks off in a fit of coughing*]

BEST MAN: [*Taking advantage of this pause*]   Ladies and gentlemen, we are gathered together, are we not, to do honour to our beloved . . .

'GENERAL': 'Let out the foretopsail-sheet, the topgallant-sail-sheet!'

BEST MAN: I was making a speech!

BRIDE'S MOTHER: We are only ignorant people, General. Tell us something funny!

BEST MAN: And brief.

'GENERAL': [*Not hearing*]   Thank you, I've had some. Did you say beef? Er, no, thanks. The old days, yes. The life on the ocean wave. [*In a voice laden with emotion*]   Tacking! Is there any joy like the joy of . . . tacking? What sailor's heart doesn't thrill to it? 'Pipe all hands on deck,' goes the cry. An electric shock runs through the crew. From captain to cabin boy . . .

MIDWIFE: I'm bored!

BEST MAN: So am I.

'GENERAL': Thank you, I've had some. Did you say pie? Er, no, thanks. [*In an exalted tone*]   All eyes on the senior officer. 'Foretopsails and mainsail braces to starboard,' he cries, 'mizzen-braces to larboard, counter-braces to port!' [*He leaps up]*   The ship rolls to the wind! 'Look alive, ye lubbers,' the officer cries, and fixes his eye on the topsail. Seconds of unbearable suspense. Then, it begins to flap! The ship begins to turn! 'Loose the stays, let go the braces,' yells the officer at the top of his voice. Then it's the tower of Babel. Things flying through the air, the old ship creaking in all its joints. *[Roaring]*   The ship is turned! *[Silence]*

BRIDE'S MOTHER: *[Furious]*   You may be a General, but you ought to be ashamed of yourself, so there!

'GENERAL': A pear? Yes, please!

BRIDE'S MOTHER: *[Louder]*   You ought to be ashamed of yourself, General or no General. *[In some confusion]*   Now, friends . . .

'GENERAL': *[Drawing himself up after hearing the* BRIDE'S MOTHER'S *second effort]*   No general. I am no general. I am a ship's captain. Equivalent to a colonel.

BRIDE'S MOTHER: No general! And you took our money! Let me tell you, sir: we don't pay good money to get ourselves insulted!

'GENERAL': *[Bewildered]*   Money? What money's that?

BRIDE'S MOTHER: You know what money. The money you took from Nyunin here. Nyunin, you made a mess of things. Engaging *this* sort of general.

INSURANCE MAN: Let's drop it. Why make a fuss?

'GENERAL': Engaged . . . money from Nyunin . . .

BRIDEGROOM: Excuse me. Didn't you accept twenty-five rubles from Mr Nyunin here?

'GENERAL': Twenty-five rubles from Nyunin . . . *[He realises]* Ah! So that's it. I see it all. *[Shaking his head sorrowfully]*   What a dirty trick, what a dirty trick!

BRIDEGROOM: At least you got paid for it.

'GENERAL': Got paid? I did NOT get paid! *[He rises from the table]*   What a trick—to insult an old man this way, a sailor, an officer who has served his country! . . . *[Muttering to himself]* If these were gentlemen, I could challenge someone to a duel, but as things are . . . *[He is distracted]*   Where is the door? Waiter, show me out, waiter! *[He is leaving]*   What a dirty trick! *[He has left]*
[Pause]

BRIDE'S MOTHER: *[To the* INSURANCE MAN*]*   So where's that twenty-five rubles?

INSURANCE MAN: The way you carry on about trifles when people are enjoying themselves! *[Loudly]*   To the happy pair! Bandmaster, a march! *[The band plays a march]*   To the happy pair!

MIDWIFE: Give me air, air! I'm suffocating here!

TELEGRAPH CLERK: [*Delighted*]   Exquisite creature!
[*Plenty of noise*]

BEST MAN: [*Trying to outshout the rest*]   Ladies and gentlemen, we are gathered together, are we not, to do honour . . .

CURTAIN

WILLIAMS
This Property is Condemned

Tennessee Williams (born 1914) is most at home in the American Deep South where he was born and reared, and the setting of his plays seldom moves very far from it, whether it is presented literally, mythically, or as an inner state of mind. It is in the damp heat and sweaty inertia of this world that the rank passions of his characters burgeon, and it is not coincidental that heat and tropical vegetation occur time and again as key images in his work. Williams is above all a poetic dramatist, but his is a poetry which is able to describe sordid reality even as it invests it with a transcendency which makes it at once compelling and curiously beautiful. It is also not solely verbal poetry: his best dramatic moments are a perfect blend of the verbal and the visual, and he employs the full resources of the theatre to give repeated poetic statement to his dominating themes of the loss of innocence, loneliness, and the final inadequacy of love itself.

Williams continually focuses attention on the psychological sufferings of people. He uses the stage to explore the innermost desires, fears and inadequacies of men and women tormented by the cruelties and deprivations inflicted on them by others, by the pressures of a brutal and impersonal society, and most of all by their own neuroses. Most of his plays are violent: their physical violence is the external manifestation of that inner emotional violence which his characters inflict on themselves and on others. He is concerned less with the major social and political issues of our day than with people: he deals with individuals in particular situations, rather than with groups in generalised ones. His dramatic obsession with violence, viciousness, selfishness and cruelty is not a sick or morbid fascination, however—it is an attempt to understand the problems of suffering humanity, and by dramatising that understanding, to make us more compassionate and so finally more human. He is neither social reformer nor objective analyst: he is as intensely involved in the problems he examines as any of his characters themselves. In an article published in the *New York Times* in 1959, before the opening of his play *Sweet Bird of Youth*, he defined the extent of his involvement:

'I think hate is a thing, a feeling, that can only exist where there is no understanding. Significantly, good physicians never have it. They never hate their patients, no matter how hateful their patients may seem to be, with their relentless, maniacal concentration upon their own tortured egos.

'Since I am a member of the human race, when I attack its behaviour towards fellow members I am obviously including myself in the attack, unless I regard myself as not human but superior to humanity. I don't. In fact, I can't expose a human weakness on the stage unless I know it through having it myself. I have exposed a good many human weaknesses and brutalities and consequently I have them.'

Although *This Property is Condemned* is a play in minor key, its insight is both sensitive and compassionate. The inherent pathos of its characters and their situation is heightened by the under-current of humour verging on the ridiculous which runs right through it. The fact that it is seen through the eyes of children serves only to make its essential problem more poignant.

CHARACTERS

WILLIE, *a young girl*   TOM, *a boy*

This Property is Condemned

SCENE: *A railroad embankment on the outskirts of a small Mississippi town on one of those milky white winter mornings peculiar to that part of the country. The air is moist and chill. Behind the low embankment of the tracks is a large yellow frame house which has a look of tragic vacancy. Some of the upper windows are boarded, a portion of the roof has fallen away. The land is utterly flat. In the left background is a bill-board that says 'GIN WITH JAKE' and there are some telephone poles and a few bare winter trees. The sky is a great milky whiteness: crows occasionally make a sound of roughly torn cloth.*

The girl WILLIE *is advancing precariously along the railroad track, balancing herself with both arms outstretched, one clutching a banana, the other an extraordinarily dilapidated doll with a frowsy blond wig.*

She is a remarkable apparition—thin as a beanpole and dressed in outrageous cast-off finery. She wears a long blue velvet party dress with a filthy cream lace collar and sparkling rhinestone beads. On her feet are battered silver kid slippers with large ornamental buckles. Her wrists and her fingers are resplendent with dimestore jewellery. She has applied rouge to her childish face in artless crimson daubs and her lips are made up in a preposterous Cupid's bow. She is about thirteen and there is something ineluctably childlike and innocent in her appearance despite the make-up. She laughs frequently and wildly and with a sort of precocious, tragic abandon.

The boy TOM, *slightly older, watches her from below the embankment. He wears corduroy pants, blue shirt and a sweater and carries a kite of red tissue paper with a gaudily ribboned tail.*

TOM: Hello. Who are you?

WILLIE: Don't talk to me till I fall off. [*She proceeds dizzily.* TOM *watches with mute fascination. Her gyrations grow wider and wider. She speaks breathlessly*]   Take my—crazy doll—will you?

TOM: [*Scrambling up the bank*]   Yeh.

WILLIE: I don't wanta—break her when—I fall! I don't think I can—stay on much—longer—do you?

TOM: Naw.

WILLIE: I'm practically—off—right now! [TOM *offers to assist her*]   No, don't touch me. It's no fair helping. You've got to do it—all—by yourself! God, I'm wobbling! I don't know what's made me so nervous! You see that water-tank way back yonder?

TOM: Yeah?

WILLIE: That's where I—started—from! This is the furthest—I ever gone—without once—falling off. I mean it will be—if I can manage to stick on—to the next—telephone—pole! Oh! Here I go! [*She becomes completely unbalanced and rolls down the bank.*]

TOM: [*Standing above her now*]   Hurtcha self?

WILLIE: Skinned my knee a little. Glad I didn't put my silk stockings on.

TOM: [*Coming down the bank*]   Spit on it. That takes the sting away.

WILLIE: Okay.

TOM: That's animal's medicine, you know. They always lick their wounds.

WILLIE: I know. The principal damage was done to my bracelet, I guess. I knocked out one of the diamonds. Where did it go?

TOM: You never could find it in all them cinders.

WILLIE: I don't know. It had a lot of shine.

TOM: It wasn't a genuine diamond.

WILLIE: How do you know?

TOM: I just imagine it wasn't. Because if it was you wouldn't be walking along a railroad track with a banged-up doll and a piece of a rotten banana.

WILLIE: Oh, I wouldn't be so sure. I might be peculiar or something. You never can tell. What's your name?

TOM: Tom.

WILLIE: Mine's Willie. We've both got boy's names.

TOM: How did that happen?

WILLIE: I was expected to be a boy but I wasn't. They had one girl already. Alva. She was my sister. Why ain't you at school?

TOM: I thought it was going to be windy so I could fly my kite.

WILLIE: What made you think that?

TOM: Because the sky was so white.

WILLIE: Is that a sign?

TOM: Yeah.

WILLIE: I know. It looks like everything had been swept off with a broom. Don't it?

TOM: Yeah.

WILLIE: It's perfectly white. It's white as a clean piece of paper.

TOM: Uh-huh.

WILLIE: But there isn't a wind.

TOM: Naw.

WILLIE: It's up too high for us to feel it. It's way, way up in the attic sweeping the dust off the furniture up there!

TOM: Uh-huh. Why ain't you at school?

WILLIE: I quituated. Two years ago this winter.

TOM: What grade was you in?

WILLIE: Five A.

TOM: Miss Preston.

WILLIE: Yep. She used to think my hands was dirty until I explained that it was cinders from falling off the railroad tracks so much.

TOM: She's pretty strict.

WILLIE: Oh, no, she's just disappointed because she didn't get married. Probably never had an opportunity, poor thing. So she has to teach Five A for the rest of her natural life. They started teaching algebra an' I didn't give a goddam what X stood for so I quit.

TOM: You'll never get an education walking the railroad tracks.

WILLIE: You won't get one flying a red kite neither. Besides . . .

TOM: What?

WILLIE: What a girl needs to get along is social training. I learned all of that from my sister Alva. She had a wonderful popularity with the railroad men.

TOM: Train engineers?

WILLIE: Engineers, firemen, conductors. Even the freight sup'rintendent. We run a boarding house for railroad men. She was I guess you might say The Main Attraction. Beautiful? Jesus, she looked like a movie star!

TOM: Your sister?

WILLIE: Yeah. One of 'em used to bring her regular after each run a great big heart-shaped red-silk box of assorted chocolates and nuts and hard candies. Marvellous?

TOM: Yeah. [*The cawing of crows sounds through the chilly air*]

WILLIE: You know where Alva is now?

TOM: Memphis?

WILLIE: Naw.

TOM: New Awleuns?

WILLIE: Naw.

TOM: St Louis?

WILLIE: You'll never guess.

TOM: Where is she then? [WILLIE *does not answer at once*]

WILLIE: [*Very solemnly*]   She's in the bone-orchard.

TOM: What?

WILLIE: [*Violently*]   Bone-orchard, cemetery, graveyard! Don't you understand English?

TOM: Sure. That's pretty tough.

WILLIE: You don't know the half of it, buddy. We used to have some high old times in that big yellow house.

TOM: I bet you did.

WILLIE: Musical instruments going all of the time.

TOM: Instruments? What kind?

WILLIE: Piano, victrola, Hawaiian steel guitar. Everyone played on something. But now it's—awful quiet. You don't hear a sound from there, do you?

TOM: Naw. Is it empty?

WILLIE: Except for me. They got a big sign stuck up.

TOM: What does it say?

WILLIE: [*Loudly but with a slight catch*] 'THIS PROPERTY IS CONDEMNED!'

TOM: You ain't still living there?

WILLIE: Uh-huh.

TOM: What happened? Where did everyone go?

WILLIE: Mama run off with a brakeman on the C. & E. I. After that everything went to pieces. [*A train whistles far off*]   You hear that whistle? That's the Cannonball Express. The fastest thing on wheels between St Louis, New Awleuns an' Memphis. My old man got to drinking.

TOM: Where is he now?

WILLIE: Disappeared. I guess I ought to refer his case to the Bureau of Missing Persons. The same as he done with Mama when she disappeared. Then there was me and Alva. Till Alva's lungs got affected. Did you see Greta Garbo in *Camille*? It played at the Delta Brilliant one time las' spring. She had the same what Alva died of. Lung affection.

TOM: Yeah?

WILLIE: Only it was—very beautiful the way she had it. You know. Violins playing. And loads and loads of white flowers. All of her lovers come back in a beautiful scene!

TOM: Yeah?

WILLIE: But Alva's all disappeared.

TOM: Yeah?

WILLIE: Like rats from a sinking ship! That's how she used to describe it. Oh, it—wasn't like death in the movies.

TOM: Naw?

WILLIE: She says, 'Where is Albert? Where's Clemence?' None of them was around. I used to lie to her, I says, 'They send their regards. They're coming to see you tomorrow.' 'Where's Mr Johnson?' she asked me. He was the freight sup'rintendent, the most important character we ever had in our rooming-house.

'He's been transferred to Grenada,' I told her. 'But wishes to be remembered.' She known I was lying.

TOM: Yeah?

WILLIE: 'This here is the pay-off!' she says. 'They all run out on me like rats from a sinking ship!' Except Sidney.

TOM: Who was Sidney?

WILLIE: The one that used to give her the great big enormous red-silk box of American Beauty choc'lates.

TOM: Oh.

WILLIE: He remained faithful to her.

TOM: That's good.

WILLIE: But she never did care for Sidney. She said his teeth was decayed so he didn't smell good.

TOM: Aw!

WILLIE: It wasn't like death in the movies. When somebody dies in the movies they play violins.

TOM: But they didn't for Alva.

WILLIE: Naw. Not even a goddam victrola. They said it didn't agree with the hospital regulations. Always singing around the house.

TOM: Who? Alva?

WILLIE: Throwing enormous parties. This was her favourite number. [*She closes her eyes and stretches out her arms in the simulated rapture of the professional blues singer. Her voice is extraordinarily high and pure with a precocious emotional timbre*]

> You're the only star
> In my blue hea-ven
> And you're shining just
> For me!

This is her clothes I got on. Inherited from her. Everything Alva's is mine. Except her solid gold beads.

TOM: What happened to them?

WILLIE: Them? She never took 'em off.

TOM: Oh!

WILLIE: I've also inherited all of my sister's beaux. Albert and Clemence and even the freight sup'rintendent.

TOM: Yeah?

WILLIE: They all disappeared. Afraid that they might get stuck for expenses I guess. But now they turn up again, all of 'em, like a bunch of bad pennies. They take me out places at night. I've got to be popular now. To parties an' dances an' all of the railroad affairs. Lookit here!

TOM: What?

WILLIE: I can do bumps! [*She stands in front of him and shoves her stomach towards him in a series of spasmodic jerks*]

TOM: Frank Waters said that . . .

WILLIE: What?

TOM: You know.

WILLIE: Know what?

TOM: You took him inside and danced for him with your clothes off.

WILLIE: Oh. Crazy Doll's hair needs washing. I'm scared to wash it though 'cause her head might come unglued where she had that compound fracture of the skull. I think that most of her brains spilled out. She's been acting silly ever since. Saying an' doing the most outrageous things.

TOM: Why don't you do that for me?

WILLIE: What? Put glue on your compound fracture?

TOM: Naw. What you did for Frank Waters.

WILLIE: Because I was lonesome then an' I'm not lonesome now. You can tell Frank Waters that. Tell him that I've inherited all of my sister's beaux. I go out steady with men in responsible jobs. The sky sure is white. Ain't it? White as a clean piece of paper. In Five A we used to draw pictures. Miss Preston would give us a piece of white foolscap an' tell us to draw what we pleased.

TOM: What did you draw?

WILLIE: I remember I drawn her a picture one time of my old man getting conked with a bottle. She thought it was good, Miss Preston, she said, 'Look here. Here's a picture of Charlie Chaplin with his hat on the side of his head!' I said, 'Aw, naw, that's not Charlie Chaplin, that's my father, an' that's not his hat, it's a bottle!'

TOM: What did she say?

WILLIE: Oh, well. You can't make a schoolteacher laugh.
              You're the only star
              In my blue hea-VEN . . .
The principal used to say there must've been something wrong with my home atmosphere because of the fact that we took in railroad men an' some of 'em slept with my sister.

TOM: Did they?

WILLIE: She was The Main Attraction. The house is sure empty now.

TOM: You ain't still living there, are you?

WILLIE: Sure.

TOM: By yourself?

WILLIE: Uh-huh. I'm not supposed to be but I am. The property is condemned but there's nothing wrong with it. Some county investigator come snooping around yesterday. I recognised her by the shape of her hat. It wasn't exactly what I would call stylish-looking.

TOM: Naw?

WILLIE: It looked like something she took off the lid of the stove. Alva knew lots about style. She had ambitions to be a designer for big wholesale firms in Chicago. She used to submit her pictures. It never worked out.

> You're the only star
> In my blue hea-ven . . .

TOM: What did you do? About the investigators?

WILLIE: Laid low upstairs. Pretended like no one was home.

TOM: Well, how do you manage to keep on eating?

WILLIE: Oh, I don't know. You keep a sharp look-out you see things lying around. This banana, perfectly good, for instance. Thrown in a garbage pail in back of the Blue Bird Café. [*She finishes the banana and tosses away the peel*]

TOM: [*grinning*]   Yeh. Miss Preston for instance.

WILLIE: Naw, not her. She gives you a white piece of paper, says 'Draw what you please!' One time I drawn her a picture of——Oh, but I told you that, huh? Will you give Frank Waters a message?

TOM: What?

WILLIE: Tell him the freight sup'rintendent has bought me a pair of kid slippers. Patent. The same as the old ones of Alva's. I'm going to dances with them at Moon Lake Casino. All night I'll be dancing an' come home drunk in the morning! We'll have serenades with all kinds of musical instruments. Trumpets an' trombones. An' Hawaiian steel guitars. Yeh! Yeh! [*She rises excitedly*]   The sky will be white like this.

TOM: [*impressed*]   Will it?

WILLIE: Uh-huh. [*She smiles vaguely and turns slowly towards him*]   White—as a clean—piece of paper . . . [*then excitedly*]   I'll draw—pictures on it!

TOM: Will you?

WILLIE: Sure!

TOM: Pictures of what?

WILLIE: Me dancing! With the freight sup'rintendent! In a pair of patent kid shoes! Yeh! Yeh! With French heels on them as high as telegraph poles! An' they'll play my favourite music!

TOM: Your favourite?

WILLIE: Yeh. The same as Alva's. [*Breathlessly, passionately*]

You're the only STAR—
In my blue HEA-VEN . . .

I'll——

TOM: What?

WILLIE: I'll—wear a corsage!

TOM: What's that?

WILLIE: Flowers to pin on your dress at a formal affair! Rosebuds! Violets! And lilies-of-the-valley! When you come home it's withered but you stick 'em in a bowl of water to freshen 'em up.

TOM: Uh-huh.

WILLIE: That's what Alva done. [*She pauses, and in the silence the train whistles*]   The Cannonball Express . . .

TOM: You think a lot about Alva. Don't you?

WILLIE: Oh, not so much. Now an' then. It wasn't like death in the movies. Her beaux disappeared. An' they didn't have violins playing. I'm going back now.

TOM: Where to, Willie?

WILLIE: The water-tank.

TOM: Yeah?

WILLIE: An' start all over again. Maybe I'll break some kind of continuous record. Alva did once. At a dance marathon in Mobile. Across the state line. Alabama. You can tell Frank Waters everything that I told you. I don't have time for inexperienced people. I'm going out now with popular railroad men, men with good salaries, too. Don't you believe me?

TOM: No. I think you're drawing an awful lot on your imagination.

WILLIE: Well, if I wanted to I could prove it. But you wouldn't be worth convincing. [*She smooths out Crazy Doll's hair*]   I'm going to live for a long, long time like my sister. An' when my lungs get affected I'm going to die like she did—maybe not like in the movies, with violins playing—but with my pearl earrings on an' my solid gold beads from Memphis. . . .

TOM: Yes?

WILLIE: [*Examining Crazy Doll very critically*]   An' then I guess——

TOM: What?

WILLIE: [*Gaily but with a slight catch*]   Somebody else will inherit all of my beaux! The sky sure is white.

TOM: It sure is.

WILLIE: White as a clean piece of paper. I'm going back now.

TOM: So long.

WILLIE: Yeh. So long. [*She starts back along the railroad track, weaving grotesquely to keep her balance. She disappears.* TOM *wets his finger and*

holds it up to test the wind. WILLIE *is heard singing from a distance*]
                          You're the only star
                          In my blue heaven—
[*There is a brief pause. The stage begins to darken*]
                          An' you're shining just—
                          For me!

                    CURTAIN

ARRABAL

The Two Executioners

Fernando Arrabal (born 1932) is a Spaniard who has lived in France since 1954 and writes in French. Though a great admirer of Beckett, he draws his main influence from that rich Spanish tradition of the grotesque which is expressed in the 'black' paintings of Goya, the surrealism of Dali, and the work of Picasso. Like them, Arrabal sees the world fragmenting as the props of its stability disintegrate one by one. In questioning the validity of traditional moral norms, Arrabal joins those who have come to believe that if reality and hope for continued existence are to be found at all, they must be sought outside the moral, social and political *status quo*, for in the mid-twentieth century these have all ceased to make sense. The century's events have tended more and more to expose the essential absence of any clear and well-defined system of beliefs and values, and writers like Arrabal have faced a universe which, because of its illogicality, has become terrifying. All previously-offered explanations of an ultimate meaning in the purpose of existence have collapsed; a scheme of values which was once familiar and comforting because it asserted an unchanging and directed order of things has for many been exposed as an illusion.

Throughout his plays, Arrabal's characters view the situation of man through the uncomprehending eyes of children. This uncomplicated simplicity becomes a powerful means of expressing his preoccupation with the inadequacy and self-contradiction of established moral and ethical rules. Since they neither perceive nor understand the existence of moral laws, his child-like characters are often cruel to one another, and like children, they suffer the cruelties and afflictions of a world whose operation they cannot comprehend, but which crushes them nevertheless.

The Two Executioners presents this world-view in a highly condensed and dramatic way. Through the eyes of two boys, Benoît and Maurice, Arrabal is able to present a blistering attack on the ambiguities of conventional morality. A mother, Françoise, is for unknown reasons determined to destroy her husband through excruciating tortures both mental and physical. Yet all the time she justifies her actions by exploiting traditionally-held beliefs about the value of religion and a mother's love, and so forces Maurice to confront an insoluble moral dilemma, in which several fundamental moral laws simultaneously contradict one another. As the final curtain falls, the play inescapably points to the essential absurdity of an ethical system which can accommodate such frightening contradictions within itself.

CHARACTERS

THE TWO EXECUTIONERS, *I don't know their names*
The Mother, FRANÇOISE
The Two Sons, BENOÎT and MAURICE
The Husband, JEAN

The Two Executioners

The action takes place in a very dark room. Left, a door opening on to the road. At the back, the door which gives on to the torture chamber. Bare walls. In the middle of the room, a table and three chairs.

[It is dark. The two EXECUTIONERS *are alone, sitting on the chairs. There is an insistent knock at the street door. It really looks as if the* EXECUTIONERS *can't hear anything. The door opens slowly, not without creaking. A woman's head appears. The woman inspects the room. She decides to come in and goes up to the* EXECUTIONERS]

FRANÇOISE: Good morning, gentlemen. . . . Excuse me. . . . Am I disturbing you?

[The EXECUTIONERS *remain motionless, as if it was nothing to do with them]*

If I'm disturbing you I'll go away. . . . *[Silence. It looks as if the woman is trying to pluck up courage. Finally she brings herself to speak and the words come tumbling out]* I came to see you because I can't stand it any longer. It's about my husband. *[Pathetically]* The being in whom I placed all my hopes, the man to whom I gave the best years of my life and whom I loved as I would never have thought I could love. *[Speaking more softly, calmer]* Yes, yes, yes, he is guilty.

[Suddenly the EXECUTIONERS *take an interest in what the woman is saying. One of them takes out a pencil and notebook]* Yes, he's guilty. He lives at number eight rue du Travail, and his name is Jean Lagune.

[The EXECUTIONER *makes a note of it. As soon as he has done so the* EXECUTIONERS *go out by the street door. A car is heard driving off.* FRANÇOISE *also goes out by the street door]*

VOICE OF FRANÇOISE: Come in, children, come in.

VOICE OF BENOÎT: There's not much light here.

VOICE OF FRANÇOISE: Yes, the room is very dark. It frightens me, but we must go in. We've got to wait for Daddy.

[Enter FRANÇOISE *and her two sons,* BENOÎT *and* MAURICE]

FRANÇOISE: Sit down, children. Don't be afraid.

[All three sit down round the table]

FRANÇOISE: *[She always speaks in a whining voice]* What sad and dramatic moments we are living through! What sins are we guilty of, that life should punish us so cruelly?

BENOÎT: Don't worry, Mother. Don't cry.

FRANÇOISE: No, my son, I'm not crying, I shan't cry, I shall stand up to all the dangers that beset us. How I love to see you always so solicitous about everything that concerns me! But just look at your brother Maurice—as unnatural as ever.

[MAURICE, *with a melancholy air, looks apparently deliberately in the opposite direction from his mother*]

Look at him; today, when more than ever I need your support, he turns against me and overwhelms me with scorn. What harm have I ever done you, unworthy son? Speak to me, say something.

BENOÎT: Don't take any notice of him, Mother, he doesn't know anything about the gratitude one owes to a mother.

FRANÇOISE: [*To Maurice*]   Can't you hear your brother? Listen to him. If anyone said such a thing to me I'd die of shame. But *you* aren't ashamed. Good God! What a cross!

BENOÎT: Gently, Mother, don't let him upset you. He'll never agree with you.

FRANÇOISE: Yes, my son, you don't realise. When it isn't your father, it's Maurice: nothing but suffering. And when I've always been their slave. Just look what a gay life so many women of my age lead, enjoying themselves night and day going to dances, cafés, cinemas! So many women! You can't realise it properly you're still too young. I could have done the same, but I preferred to sacrifice myself for my husband and for you, silently, humbly, without expecting anything from my sacrifices, and even knowing that one day the beings who have been the dearest to me would say what your brother says today—that I haven't done enough. Can you see, my son, how they reward my sacrifices? You can see—by always returning evil for good, always.

BENOÎT: How good you are! How good you are!

FRANÇOISE: But what good does it do me to know that? It comes to the same thing. Everything comes to the same thing. I don't feel like doing anything any more, I don't care about anything, nothing is important to me any more. I just want to be good and always sacrifice myself for you, without expecting anything for my sacrifices, and even knowing that one day the beings who have been the dearest to me, those who ought to be grateful for all my concern for them, deliberately ignore my sacrifices. All my life I've been a martyr to you, and I shall continue to be a martyr until God chooses to recall me to Him.

BENOÎT: Dearest Mother!

FRANÇOISE: Yes, my son, I live only for you. How can I have any other interests? Luxury, dresses, parties, the theatre—none of these count for me, I have but one care: you. What does the rest matter?

BENOÎT: [*To* MAURICE]   Maurice, do you hear what Mother says?

FRANÇOISE: Let him be, my child. Do you think I can hope that he will be able to recognise my sacrifices? No. I expect nothing from him. I even know that he probably thinks that I haven't done enough.

BENOÎT: [*To* MAURICE]   You're a good-for-nothing.

FRANÇOISE: [*Excited*]   Don't make things worse for me, Benoît, don't pick a quarrel with him. I want us to live in peace, in harmony. Whatever happens I don't want you brothers to quarrel.

BENOÎT: How good you are, Mother! . . . and good to him when he's so worthless. If it weren't for the fact that you ask me to spare him, I don't know what I'd do to him. [*To* MAURICE, *aggressively*] You can say thank you to Mother, Maurice, because you deserve a good thrashing.

FRANÇOISE: No, my child, no, don't hit him. I don't want you to hit him even if he does thoroughly deserve it. I want peace and love to reign in our midst. That's the only thing I ask of you, Benoît.

BENOÎT: Don't worry, I'll do what you ask.

FRANÇOISE: Thank you, my son. You are like balm for the injuries that life has inflicted upon me. You see, God in his infinite goodness has finally granted me a son like you to bind up the wounds my poor heart suffers, the grief caused me, to my great distress, by the beings I have struggled for the most: my husband and Maurice.

BENOÎT: [*Angrily*]   From now on, no one shall make you suffer any more.

FRANÇOISE: Don't be angry, my son, don't be upset. They've behaved badly, and they know it. What we must do is forgive them, and bear them no malice. And anyway, even though your father has sinned, sinned greatly even, you must nonetheless respect him.

BENOÎT: Respect him: *him?*

FRANÇOISE: Yes, my son. You must disregard all the suffering he has caused. It is I who should refuse him my forgiveness, and you see, my son, I forgive him, although he has made me suffer more than I have suffered before, if that is possible, I shall continue to wait for him with open arms and I shall be able to forgive him his innumerable faults. Ever since the day I was born, life has taught me how to suffer. But I carry this cross with dignity, out of love for you.

BENOÎT: Mother, you're so good!

FRANÇOISE: [*In an even more humble tone*]   I try, Benoît, to be good.

BENOÎT: [*Interrupting his mother with a gesture of spontaneous affection*]   Mother, you are the best woman in the world.

FRANÇOISE: [*Humble and ashamed*]   No, my son, I am not the best woman in the world, I cannot aspire to such a claim, I am too unworthy. And then, I have probably committed some sins. In spite of a great deal of good will; but even so, what counts is that I have committed some sins.

BENOÎT: [*With conviction*]   No, Mother; never.

FRANÇOISE: Yes, my child, sometimes. But I can say with joy that I have always repented of them—always.

BENOÎT: You are a saint.

FRANÇOISE: Hush! What more beautiful dream could I have than saintliness! I can't be a saint. To be a saint one must be a very great person, but I am worth nothing. I simply try to be good—that is the limit of my pretensions.

[*The street door opens. Enter the two* EXECUTIONERS, *carrying Jean, Françoise's husband, who has his feet and wrists tied together and is hanging from a big stick, rather after the fashion in which captured lions or tigers are carried in Africa. Jean is gagged; as he is brought into the room he raises his head and looks at his wife,* FRANÇOISE, *opening his eyes very widely and perhaps with some anger.* FRANÇOISE *looks at her husband attentively, avidly even.* MAURICE *watches the procession go by with violent indignation. The two* EXECUTIONERS, *without stopping, cross the room and carry* JEAN *from the street door into the torture chamber. All three disappear*]

MAURICE: [*To his mother, very indignantly*]   What's going on? What's the latest dirty trick?

BENOÎT: [*To* MAURICE]   Don't talk to Mother like that.

FRANÇOISE: Let him be, my child, let him insult me. Let him reproach me. Let him treat his mother like an enemy. Let him be, my child, let him be, God will punish this wicked action.

MAURICE: Oh, that's *too* much. [*Angrily, to his mother*]   It was you who denounced him.

BENOÎT: [*Ready to throw himself on his brother*]   I've already told you to speak civilly to Mother. D'you understand? Civilly! D'you hear me?

FRANÇOISE: Gently, my son, gently, let him be rude to me. You know very well that he's only happy when he's making me suffer; give him that satisfaction. That's my job—to sacrifice myself for him and for you; to give you everything you want.

BENOÎT: I won't let him shout at you.

FRANÇOISE: Obey me, my son, obey me.

BENOÎT: I won't obey you. You're too good and he takes advantage of it.

[MAURICE *looks dejected*]

FRANÇOISE: My child, do you too want to make me suffer? If he is unpleasant to me, let him be unpleasant, it was only to be expected, but you, my son, you are different—at least that's what I've always thought. Let him torture me if it does his evil heart any good.

BENOÎT: No, never; not when I'm there, at any rate.

[*The sounds of a whip can be heard followed by cries muffled by the gag. It is* JEAN. *The* EXECUTIONERS *are, no doubt, flogging him in the torture chamber.* FRANÇOISE *and* MAURICE *get up and go over to the torture chamber door. The mother listens avidly, her eyes wide open, a grimace on her face (almost a smile?), hysterical. The sounds of the whip become louder for a long moment.* JEAN *groans loudly. At last the sounds of the whip and the cries cease.*]

MAURICE: [*Furiously, and on the verge of tears, to his mother*]   It's your fault that they're whipping Daddy. It was you who denounced him.

BENOÎT: Shut up! [*Violently*]   Don't take any notice, Mother.

FRANÇOISE: Let him be, let him be, Benoît. Let him insult me. I know very well that if you weren't there he would hit me. But he's a coward and he's afraid of you, that's the only thing that stops him, because he is quite capable of lifting his hand against his mother, I can read it in his eyes. He's always been trying to.

[*A piercing moan from* JEAN. *Silence.* FRANÇOISE *makes a grimace which is almost a smile. Silence*]

Let's go and see poor little Daddy. Let's go and see him suffering, the poor man. Because there's no doubt about it, they must have hurt him a lot. [*Grimaces from* FRANÇOISE. *Silence.* FRANÇOISE *approaches the torture chamber, half-opens the door, and, standing by the door, looks into the room. Talking to her husband, who is in the room and so can't see her*]   They must have hurt you a lot, Jean. Poor Jean! You must have suffered so much, and they're going to make you suffer even more. My poor Jean!

[JEAN, *though impeded by the gag, cries out in anger*]

Don't get into a state. It'd be better to try to be patient. You must realise that you're only at the beginning of your sufferings. You can't do anything at the moment, you're tied up, and your back's covered with blood. You can't do anything. Just calm down! And anyway, all this is going to do you a lot of good, it'll teach you to have some will power—you never did have any. [FRANÇOISE *decides to go into the room; she does so, i.e. she goes off-stage*]

VOICE OF FRANÇOISE: [*Speaking as if she were at church, but out loud*]   It was I who denounced you, Jean. It was I who said you were guilty.

[JEAN *tries to speak, but as he is hindered by his gag he can only manage to make noises.* FRANÇOISE'S *abnormal laugh can be heard.* MAURICE *is very worked up.* FRANÇOISE *reappears*]

FRANÇOISE: [*To her sons*]   The poor man is suffering a lot, he hasn't any patience, he never did have any.

[*Cry from* JEAN]

MAURICE: Leave Daddy alone. Don't go on. Can't you see you're tormenting him?

FRANÇOISE: It's he who's tormenting himself; only he, and for no reason. [*She again addresses her husband through the door*]   I can see very well that it's you who are tormenting yourself. I can see very well that what I say irritates you. [*Pause—smile*]   Who could pay more attention to your sufferings than I do? I shall be at your side every time you suffer. You're guilty, and it's your duty to accept your punishment with patience. You even ought to thank the executioners for taking so much trouble with you. If you were a normal, humble, just man, you'd thank the executioners, but you've always been a rebel. You needn't think you're at home now, at home where you did everything you wanted to; at the moment you're in the executioners' power. Accept your punishment without rebelling. It's your purification. Repent your sins, and promise that you won't fall back into error. And don't torment yourself with the thought that I am rejoicing to see you punished.

[*Loud groan from* JEAN]

MAURICE: Can't you hear him groaning? Can't you see you're making him suffer? Leave him in peace!

BENOÎT: I've already told you not to talk to Mother like that.

FRANÇOISE: Let him talk to me as he wishes, my son. I'm used to it. It's my lot: to worry about them, about him and about Daddy, though they don't deserve it, and though no one thanks me for it.

[*Groans from* JEAN]

MAURICE: Daddy! Daddy! [*On the verge of tears*]   Daddy!

FRANÇOISE: He's still groaning. That's a sign that he's suffering from the wounds caused by the whip and the ropes fastening his hands and feet. [*She opens the drawer in the table and searches about inside it. Then she puts on the table a bottle of vinegar and a salt cellar which she has found in it*]   These are just what I need. I'll put vinegar and salt on his wounds to disinfect them. A bit of vinegar and salt on his wounds will do wonders! [*With hysterical enthusiasm*]   A bit of salt and vinegar. Only just a tiny bit on each wound, that's all he needs.

MAURICE: [*Angrily*]   Don't do that.

FRANÇOISE: Is that the way you love your father? You, his favourite son, is that how you treat him? You, you of all people, wicked son! You who know very well that the executioners will flog him until death results, are you going to abandon him now and not even let me bandage his wounds? [FRANÇOISE *goes towards the torture chamber with the vinegar and salt in her hand*]

MAURICE: Don't put salt on him! If they're going to kill him anyway, at least leave him in peace, don't make the agony worse.

FRANÇOISE: You're very young, my son, you don't know anything about life, you haven't any experience. What would have become of you without me? Life has always been very easy for you. You're used to your mother giving you everything you want. You must remember what I say. I speak as a mother, and a mother lives only for her children. Respect your mother, respect her, if only for the white hairs which adorn her brow. Think that your mother does everything for you out of affection. When, my son, have you ever seen your mother do anything for herself? I have thought only of you. First my children, and then my husband. I don't count, not for anybody, and even less for myself. That is why, my son, now that I am going to take care of your father's wounds, you mustn't stand in my way. Others would kiss the ground I tread on. I don't ask so much from you, I merely hope that you may find it in you to thank me for my efforts. [*Pause.* FRANÇOISE *goes towards the torture chamber with the salt and vinegar*]   I'll go and put a little salt and vinegar on poor little Daddy's wounds.

[MAURICE *seizes his mother's arm brutally and prevents her from going into the room*]

BENOÎT: Don't hold Mother's arm!

FRANÇOISE: Let him hit me. It's what he's always wanted. Look at the marks of his fingers on my poor arm. That's what he's always wanted to do—hit me.

BENOÎT: [*Very angry*]   How dare you hit Mother?

[BENOÎT *tries to hit his brother.* FRANÇOISE *throws herself between her sons to stop them fighting*]

FRANÇOISE: No, my son, not in my presence. The family is sacred. I don't want my sons to fight.

[BENOÎT *controls himself with difficulty*]

He can flay me alive if he wants to, but *please*, my child, don't hit him in my presence. I don't want any quarrels between brothers in my presence. He has hit me; but I forgive him.

[*Loud cry from her husband*]

He is suffering—they are making him suffer. . . . He's suffering a great deal. I must put some vinegar on him as quickly as possible. At once. [FRANÇOISE *goes into the torture chamber*]

VOICE OF FRANÇOISE: Just a little salt and vinegar will do you a lot of good. Don't move, I haven't got much. There, there we are.

[*Groan from* JEAN]

That's it, there, there, now a bit of salt.

[*Angry cry from* JEAN]

MAURICE: [*Shouts*] Daddy! [*And weeps*]

VOICE OF FRANÇOISE: That's it, just a tiny bit more, there, a tiny bit more, don't move. [FRANÇOISE *speaks in gasps*]   Don't move. There. Just a bit more.

[*Groan from* JEAN]

That's it, just a bit more; there, there it'll do you good.

[*Cry from* JEAN]

Just to finish it up, there.

[*Cry from* JEAN]

VOICE OF FRANÇOISE: That's all I've got!

[*Long silence. Cry from* JEAN. *Silence*]

Well now, how are your sore places? I'll touch them to see how they are.

[*Loud cry from* JEAN. MAURICE, *when his brother isn't looking, goes into the room*]

VOICE OF MAURICE: What are you doing? You're scratching his wounds!

[MAURICE *pushes his mother out of the room.* BENOÎT *throws himself on to his brother, about to hit him. The mother comes between them and separates the brothers*]

FRANÇOISE: No, my son, no. [*To* BENOÎT]   You're hurting *me*, not him! No, don't hit your brother. I don't want you to hit him.

[BENOÎT *calms down*]

BENOÎT: I won't tolerate him hurting you.

FRANÇOISE: Yes, let him hurt me. Let him if he enjoys it. That's what he wants. Let him. He wants me to cry when he hits me.

My son, that's how your brother's made. What a martyr! What a cross! Why, O God, have I deserved to have a son who doesn't love me and who is only waiting for me to have a moment of weakness to beat and torment me!

BENOÎT: [*Furious*]   Maurice!

FRANÇOISE: Gently, my son, gently. [*Dejected*]   What a cross! What a cross, O God! Why do you punish me thus, Lord? What have I done to provoke such a punishment? Don't fight, my children, for the sake of your poor mother who never ceases to suffer, for the sake of her white hairs. [*To* BENOÎT]   And if *he* won't take pity on my sufferings, you at least, Benoît, must have pity on me and not make me suffer. Or can it be that you don't love me either?

[BENOÎT, *moved, tries to say something. His mother doesn't let him speak, and continues*]

Yes, that's it, you don't love me either.

BENOÎT: [*On the verge of tears*]   Yes Mother, I do—I love you.

FRANÇOISE: Well then, why do you add extra thorns to the crown of sorrows I bear?

BENOÎT: Mother!

FRANÇOISE: Don't you see my sorrow? Don't you see the boundless sorrow of a mother?

BENOÎT: [*Nearly crying*]   Yes.

FRANÇOISE: Thank you, my son, you are the support of my old age. You are the unique consolation that God has given me in this life.

[*The* EXECUTIONERS *can again be heard whipping* JEAN. *The husband sobs. All three,* FRANÇOISE *and her sons, listen in silence*]

FRANÇOISE: They're beating him again. . . . And they must be hurting him a lot. . . . [FRANÇOISE *speaks in gasps*]   He's crying! He's crying. . . . He's groaning, isn't he? [*No one answers*]   . . . Yes, yes, he's groaning, he's groaning, I can hear him perfectly. . . .

[*Sounds of the whip, and groans.* JEAN *suddenly gives a more piercing cry. The* EXECUTIONERS *continue their blows.* JEAN *doesn't groan any more.* FRANÇOISE *goes to the door and looks into the room*]

They've killed him! They've killed him!

[*Absolute silence.* MAURICE *sits down, puts his head on the table. He is crying perhaps. Silence. Long pause. Enter the two* EXECUTIONERS *with Jean, tied up as before.* JEAN *is dead. His head hangs down inertly*]

FRANÇOISE: [*To the* EXECUTIONERS]   Let me see him. Let me see him properly.

[*The* EXECUTIONERS, *without paying any attention to* FRANÇOISE, *cross the room and go out by the street door.* FRANÇOISE *and* BENOÎT *sit down on either side of* MAURICE. *They look at him. Silence*]

MAURICE: [*To* FRANÇOISE]   They killed Daddy because of you.

FRANÇOISE: How dare you say that to your mother? To your mother who has always taken so much trouble with you.

MAURICE: [*Interrupting her*]   Don't give me all that stuff. What I'm accusing you of is of denouncing Daddy.

[BENOÎT *is too depressed to intervene*]

FRANÇOISE: Yes, my son, as you wish. If it gives you any pleasure I'll say it was my fault. Is that what you want?

MAURICE: Oh, stop harping on that. [*Pause. Long silence*]   Why did you treat Daddy like that, Daddy who never gave you anything to complain of?

FRANÇOISE: That's it. That's what I've been waiting for, all my life. When your father compromised the future of his children and his wife because of his. . . .

MAURICE: [*Interrupting her*]   What's all that stuff about compromising the future? What's your latest invention?

FRANÇOISE: Ah, my son! What misery! What a cross! [*Pause*]   Of course he compromised his children's future by his failings. He knew very well that if he continued in his guilty ways he would sooner or later finish up the way he has. He knew it only too well, but he didn't change, he continued, whatever happened, on his guilty way. How many times did I tell him so! How many times did I tell him: you're going to leave me a widow and your sons orphans. But what did he do? He ignored my advice and persisted in the error of his ways.

MAURICE: You're the only one who says he was guilty.

FRANÇOISE: Ah yes, naturally, you're not content now with having insulted me all night long, but you're going to call me a liar as well and swear that I make people perjure themselves. That's the way you treat a mother who, ever since you were born, has given you all her care and attention. While your father was compromising your future with his misbehaviour, I was thinking of your happiness and I had only one aim—to make you happy, to give you all the happiness that I had never known. Because for me, the only thing that counts is that your brother and you should be all right, everything else was of no importance. I'm a poor, ignorant, uneducated woman, who wants nothing but the good of her children, whatever the cost.

BENOÎT: [*Conciliatingly*]   Maurice, there isn't any point in making a fuss now; Daddy's dead, we can't do anything about it now.

FRANÇOISE: Benoît's right.

[*Long silence*]

MAURICE: We could have prevented Daddy's death.

FRANÇOISE: How? Was it my fault? No. He was the one who was guilty—he, your father. What could I do? What could I do to stop him being like that? He'd got stubborn. I'm only a poor, ignorant, uneducated woman, I've spent my whole life doing nothing but worrying about other people, forgetting myself. When have you seen me buy a pretty dress or go to the cinema or to first nights, which I used to like so much? No, I didn't do any of those things, in spite of all the pleasure I'd have got out of them, and that was only because I preferred to devote myself entirely to you. I only ask one thing—that you shouldn't be ungrateful, and that you should be capable of appreciating the sacrifice of a mother like the one you were lucky enough to have.

BENOÎT: Yes, Mother, *I* appreciate all you've done for us.

FRANÇOISE: Yes, I know *you* do, but your brother doesn't. It doesn't seem anything to your brother, it isn't enough for him. How happy we could be if only we were all united, if only we all agreed!

BENOÎT: Maurice, yes, we ought to understand one another and all three live in peace. Mother is very good, I know she loves you very much and that she'll give you everything you need. Even if it's only out of selfishness, come back to us. We'll all three live happily and joyfully together and love one another.

MAURICE: But . . . [*Pause*]   Daddy . . .

[*Silence*]

BENOÎT: That's already past history. Don't look backwards. What matters is the future. It would be too stupid to hang on to the past. You'll have everything you want with mother. Everything that's hers will be yours. Isn't that so, Mother?

FRANÇOISE: Yes, my son, everything that is mine will be his; I forgive him.

BENOÎT: You see how good she is; she even forgives you.

FRANÇOISE: Yes, I forgive you, and I shall forget all your insults.

BENOÎT: She'll forget everything! [*Gaily*]   That's the important thing. And so we'll all three live together without ill-feeling; Mother, you, and me. What could be more wonderful?

MAURICE: [*Half convinced*]   Yes, but . . .

BENOÎT: [*Interrupting him*]   No, you mustn't be vindictive. Be like Mother. She has reason to be angry with you, but she's promised to forget everything. We shall be happy if you'll be nice.

[MAURICE, *full of emotion, lowers his head. Long silence.* BENOÎT *puts his arm round his brother*]

Kiss Mother.

[*Silence*]

Kiss her and let bygones be bygones.

[MAURICE *goes up to his mother and kisses her*]

FRANÇOISE: My son!

BENOÎT: [*To* MAURICE]   Ask Mother to forgive you.

MAURICE: [*Nearly crying*]   Forgive me, Mother.

[MAURICE *and* FRANÇOISE *embrace.* BENOÎT *joins them and all three stay enfolded in each other's arms while the curtain falls*]

CURTAIN

O'CASEY

The End of the Beginning

Sean O'Casey (born 1884) in his first plays proved himself a worthy successor to the great dramatists of the Irish 'Renaissance', Yeats, Lady Gregory and Synge. But he was not simply a follower: though he owed his origin and most formative influence to this movement, he added to it and expanded its scope. Yeats had brought poetry to the Irish stage, Lady Gregory had been its main political voice, and Synge had offered a critically realistic portrait of its peasants. O'Casey initially began by examining the lower-class life of the city—Dublin, his birthplace. To this examination he added both poetry and political concern, for he too possessed in remarkable measure the dramatic gifts of his predecessors: a rich sense of language, a keen and critical insight into character, and a sure ability to transform inherently dramatic material into tightly-knit plays. His earliest plays, firmly realistic in form, took their themes from the tense and passionate events of Ireland's troubled political life, and he subjected his characters to the same incisive critical scrutiny that Synge had done. It was no doubt as gratifying to him as it had been to the others when his plays also provoked a storm of controversy. But in his case, to the riots and near-hysterical critical attacks from the public, the press and the church, with which the directors of Dublin's Abbey Theatre were long familiar, was added the outrage of the actors themselves against the "filthy, blasphemous" things they had to say.

The End of the Beginning is a play typical of the early O'Casey. Through hilarious comedy, he pointedly satirises the ancient struggle for dominance between men and women, in a milieu as typically Irish as its relevance is universal. The play gains in point from its highly realistic presentation: no place could be more appropriate than a kitchen for the proper battlefield in the war of the sexes, just as no victory could be finally more Pyrrhic in the narrow confines of a home. In times when the Women's Liberation movement grows ever more demanding, O'Casey's play might suggest that women are in fact asking for that which they have always had.

CHARACTERS

DARRY BERRILL: *About fifty-five; stocky, obstinate, with a pretty big belly. He is completely bald, except for a tuft of grey hair just above the forehead.*

BARRY DERRILL: *Darry's neighbour. Same age as Darry. Thin, easy-going, big moustache, and is very near-sighted.*

LIZZIE BERRILL: *Darry's wife. About forty-five. A good woman about the house, but that's about all.*

The End of the Beginning

A big, comfortable kitchen. Steep stairs, almost like a ladder, leading to upper room, top right. Huge fireplace, right. Some chairs, one heavy, with rubbered castors. Small settee, and table. Chest of drawers, left, on top of which stands a gramophone. Door back, and to left of door a window. To right of door, a dresser, on which is, as well as delf, a large clock of the alarm type. To right of dresser, on a nail, hangs a whip; to the left of dresser hangs a mandolin. On table, a quantity of unwashed delf. To right of fireplace, a lumber room. The room, at night, is lighted by an electric bulb, hanging from centre of ceiling. It is a fine early autumn evening, with the sun low in the heavens. On wall, back, a large red card on which 'Do It Now' is written in white letters. A sink under the window.

DARRY: [*At door of room above. He is shaving, and his chin is covered with lather*] This shaving water's dead cold, woman. D'ye hear me? This shaving water's dead cold.

LIZZIE: [*Busy about the room—quietly*] Come down and heat it, then.

DARRY: [*Scornfully*] Too much to do, I suppose. I'd do all that has to be done here, three times over, 'n when all was finished, I'd be sighing for something to do.

LIZZIE: If you had half of what I have to do here, at the end of the evening you'd be picked up dead out of the debris.

DARRY: I would?

LIZZIE: You would.

DARRY: Sure?

LIZZIE: Certain.

DARRY: If I only had half to do?

LIZZIE: Or less.

DARRY: I'd be picked up out of the debris?

LIZZIE: Out of the middle of it.

DARRY: Dead?

LIZZIE: As a mackerel.

DARRY: [*Fiercely*] I'm always challenging you to change places for a few hours, but you won't do it. I'd show you what a sinecure of a job you had here, while I'm sweating out in the fields.

LIZZIE: Go out 'n finish the mowing of the meadow. It'll take you only half an hour or so, 'n there's plenty of light in the sky still.

DARRY: [*Who has been shaving himself during this argument*]   The meadow'll do to be done tomorrow. Why don't you let me do what's to be done in the house, an' you go 'n mow the meadow? Why don't you do that? 'don't you do that? 'you do that? Agony to look at you; agony to listen to you; agony, agony to be anywhere near you.

LIZZIE: I'd just like to see you doing what's to be done about the house—I'd just like to see you.

DARRY: What is there to be done about the house—will you tell us that?

LIZZIE: There's the pig 'n the heifer 'n the hens to be fed 'n tended. There's ironing, cooking, washing, 'n sewing to be done.

DARRY: Sewing! An' only a button back 'n front of me so that it's the next thing to a miracle that my trousers are kept from starting the neighbours talking.

LIZZIE: If you say much more, I'll go 'n mow the meadow, 'n leave you to see what you can make of the house-work.

DARRY: [*Angrily*]   Buzz off, buzz off, then, an' I'll show you how the work of a house is done. Done quietly; done with speed, 'n without a whisper of fuss in its doing. Buzz off, if you want to, 'n I'll show you 'n all your sex how the work of a house is done!

[LIZZIE *violently pulls off a jazz-coloured overall she is wearing, and flings it on the floor*]

LIZZIE: [*Furiously*]   Put that on you, 'n do what remains to be done about the house, while I go an' mow the meadow. Get into it, 'n show the world an' your poor wife the wonders you can do when you're under a woman's overall.

DARRY: [*A little frightened*]   Oh, I'll manage all right.

LIZZIE: An' don't you let that Alice Lanigan in here while I'm away either, d'ye hear?

DARRY: What Alice Lanigan?

LIZZIE: [*In a temper*]   What Alice Lanigan! The Alice Lanigan I caught you chattering to yesterday, when you should have been mowing the meadow. The Alice Lanigan that's setting you on to nag at me about the little I have to do in the house. The Alice Lanigan that's goading you into the idea that if you were a little slimmer round the belly, you'd be a shevaleer, an's getting you to do physical jerks. The Alice Lanigan that's on the margin of fifty, 'n assembles herself together as if she was a girl in her teens, jutting out her bust when she's coming in, 'n jutting out her behind when she's going out, like the Lady of Shalott, to catch the men—that's the Alice Lanigan I mean.

DARRY: I don't be thinking of Alice Lanigan.

LIZZIE: I've seen you, when you thought I slumbered 'n slept, naked, with nothing at all on you, doing your physical jerks in front of the looking-glass, 'n that too, when the lessons of a Mission were still hot in your heart—an' all for Alice Lanigan. Maybe you don't know that she has a kid who has never had a pat on the head from a father.

DARRY: You buzz off now, 'n I'll show how the work of a house is done.

LIZZIE: [*While she is putting a broad-brimmed hat on her head, pulling a pair of old gloves over her hands, and taking down a whip hanging from a nail in the wall*]   I'm telling you it's a dangerous thing to shake hands with Alice Lanigan, even with a priest giving the introduction. The day'll come soon when you'll know she's making mechanical toys of you 'n that other old fool, Barry Derrill, who's so near-sighted that he can't see the sky, unless the moon's shining in it!

DARRY: Cheerio.

LIZZIE: [*At the door*]   I'm going now, 'n we'll see how you do the work of the house.

DARRY: Hail 'n farewell to you. An' mind you, this'll be only the beginning of things.

LIZZIE: God grant that it won't be the end, an' that when I come back, I'll at least find the four walls standing.

[*She goes out.* DARRY *strolls to the door, and watches her going down the road*]

DARRY: [*Scornfully to himself*]   Mow the meadow! Well, let her see her folly out.

[*As he shuts the door, the clock in the distant Town Hall strikes eight.* DARRY *returns, glances at the clock on the dresser, notices that it has stopped, takes it up, puts his ear against it, shakes it, begins to wind it, finds it difficult to turn, puts added strength into the turning, and a whirring rattle, like a strong spring breaking, comes from the inside of the clock. He hastily replaces the clock on the dresser. After a few seconds' thought, he takes it up again, removes the back, and part of a big, broken spring darts out, which he hurriedly crams in again, and puts the clock back on the dresser.*]

DARRY: Lizzie again!

[*He catches sight of the gramophone, looks at it, thinks for a second, goes over to the chest of drawers, takes some records from behind it, and fixes one on the disc of the gramophone. He takes off his waistcoat, loosens his braces, stands stiff, strokes his thighs, pats his belly, and tries to push it back a little. He starts the gramophone going, runs to the centre of the room, and lies down on the broad of his back. The gramophone begins to give directions for physical exercises, to which* DARRY *listens and, awkwardly, clumsily, and puffingly, tries to follow the movements detailed in the words spoken by the gramophone when the music commences*]

GRAMOPHONE: Lie on back; hand behind the head; feet together—are you ready? Bend the right knee; draw it into the waistline, towards the chest—commence!

[DARRY *is too slow, or the gramophone is too quick, for he can't keep up with the time of the music. When he finds that he is behind the time of the music,* DARRY *increases his speed by partial performance of the movements, and so gets into touch with the time, but presently, blowing and panting, he is out of time again by a beat or two. He climbs stiffly on to his feet, goes over to gramophone and puts the indicator to 'Slow'*]

DARRY: Phuh. Too quick, too damn quick altogether

[*He starts the gramophone going, runs to the centre of the room, and again lies down on the broad of his back. When the music begins he goes through the movements as before; but the music is playing so slowly now that he finds it impossible to go slowly enough to keep to the time of the tune. When he finds himself in front of a beat he stops and puffs and waits for the beat to catch up with him before he recommences. As he is going through these movements, the door opens, and* BARRY DERRILL *comes into the room. He has a mandolin under his arm, and is wearing wide-rimmed, thick-lensed spectacles.*]

BARRY: [*Briskly*] Come 'n kiss me sweet 'n twenty what the hell are you trying to do?

DARRY: Can't you see what I'm trying to do? Take off your spectacles 'n get a closer look. Keeping meself fit 'n flexible—that's what I'm trying to do.

BARRY: The rhythm's too slow, man; tense your muscles, you're not tun'd into the movements properly, man.

DARRY: The indicator must have shifted. Slip over 'n put it to the point marked medium, 'n then get down here 'n give us a hand.

BARRY: What about the prologue of playing the song we're to sing at the Town Hall concert?

DARRY: Get down 'n have five minutes of this, first; we'll both sing the better for it.

BARRY: [*Dubiously*] Never done it to music, 'n I wouldn't be able to keep in touch with the—with the measure.

DARRY: The music makes it easier, man. Keep your eye on me, 'n move when I move.

[BARRY *reluctantly takes off his coat and waistcoat, goes over to the gramophone, puts his nose against the instrument, and puts the indicator to 'Fast'*]

DARRY: To do this thing properly you'd want to be wearing shorts. Right; now keep in touch with the rhythm, or you'll mar everything. Start her off, and stretch yourself down.

[BARRY *starts the gramophone, runs over and lies down opposite to* DARRY, *so that the soles of their feet are only a few inches apart*]

GRAMOPHONE: [*Very rapidly*] Lie on back; hands behind the head; feet together—are you ready? Bend the right knee; draw it into the waistline towards the chest; breathe out—commence!

[*The tempo of the tune forces them to do the exercises in a frantic way, till it dawns on* DARRY, *who is nearly exhausted, that there's something wrong. He stops while* BARRY *goes on manfully*]

DARRY: [*Scornfully*] Eh, eh, there, wait a minute, wait a minute, man. Don't you see anything wrong?

BARRY: [*Stopping*] No; what's wrong?

DARRY: [*Testily*] Aw, what's wrong! We're congestin' ourselves with speed; that's what's wrong. You must have jammed the indicator hard to Fast. [*He gets up, goes to the gramophone, and puts it right.*] We're entertainin' ourselves, an' not tryin' to say the Rosary.

[*He comes back and stretches himself again on the floor. The music begins and the two men commence the exercises. After a few moments,* DARRY *slows down a little, misses several beats, and tries to blame* BARRY]

DARRY: [*Excitedly keeping up the movements, but out of time, as he talks*] Try to keep the proper rhythm up, man. [*He hums the tune of 'Coming thro' the Rye'*] Dad th' didee dah th' diddy dah th' diddy dee—that way, man. Dah, th' diddy day th' diddy [*Rapidly*] Keep your eye on me. Dah th' diddy dee.

[*After a few moments* DARRY *is out of time and breathless; he stops and sits up to complain, but he really wants to get a rest*]

DARRY: [*With aggravated patience*] Barry, you're spoiling the whole thing by getting out of time. Don't let your arms and legs go limber, tense your muscles. Three beats to the bar, see? Now!

[*They start again;* DARRY *is soon behind time, blowing and puffing out of him.* BARRY *keeps to the beat of the tune splendidly*]

DARRY: [*Angrily*] You're going too damn quick altogether, now, man!

BARRY: No I'm not—I'm there to the tick every time.

DARRY: [*Violently*] There to the tick—how is it you're not in the line with me, then, if you're there to the tick? I don't know whether you're in front of me or behind me. Are you too stiff or what?

BARRY: I'm there to the second every time. It's you that's missin' a beat in the bar.

DARRY: [*Indignantly, stopping to talk, while* BARRY *goes on*] I'm missin' it because I'm trying to foster you into the right balance 'n rhythm of the movements. That's why I'm missin' it. [*Loudly*]   An' I'm wastin' me time!

BARRY: [*Sharply*]   I'm doin' me best, amn't I?

DARRY: [*More sharply still*]   Your best's a hell of a way behind what's wanted. It's pitiful 'n painful to be watchin' you, man. [*He stands up and looks at* BARRY, *who keeps going*] Eh, eh, you'll do yourself an injury, Barry. Get up 'n we'll do the song. [*As* BARRY *goes on*] Oh, get up 'n we'll do the song.

[BARRY *gets up reluctantly, and* DARRY *goes over and stops the gramophone*]

BARRY: I was doin' it well enough, if you'd let me alone.

DARRY: [*Scornfully*]   Yes; like the Londonderry Air play'd in march time.

[*They get their mandolins and stand side by side at the back*]

DARRY: Now we walk in a semicircle down to the front, 'n bow, you remember? Ready?

BARRY: Yep.

DARRY: Go!

[*They both step off to the right, take a few steps, and then they halt*]

BARRY: Something wrong; we don't go round the same way, do we?

DARRY: [*Testily*]   Of course there's something wrong; of course we don't go round the same way. Can't you try to remember, Barry? You're to go to the left, to the left.

BARRY: I remember distinctly I was to go to the right.

DARRY: [*Irritably*]   Oh, don't be such an egoist, Barry. Now think for a minute. [*A pause*]   Now make up your mind—d'ye want to go to the left or the right?

BARRY: [*Testily*]   Oh, left, right—any way.

DARRY: Left, then. Go.

[*They march round, one to the right, the other to the left, meet in the front, and bow*]

DARRY: You start, Barry, my boy.

BARRY: [*Singing*]

One summer eve a handsome man met a handsome maiden strolling,

DARRY:

Down where the bees were hummin' an' the wild flowers gaily growing:

BARRY:

Said she. We'll sit down here a while, all selfish thoughts controlling,

DARRY:

Down where the bees are hummin' an' the wild flowers gaily growing:

BARRY:

Said she, We'll meditate on things, things high 'n edifying,

How all things live 'n have their day 'n end their day by dying.

He put his hand on her white breast an' murmur'd, Life is trying,

DARRY:

Down where the bees are hummin' an' the wild flowers gaily growing.

BARRY:

The moon glanc'd down 'n wonder'd what the pair of them were doing,

DARRY:

Down where the bees were hummin' an' the wild flowers gaily growing;

BARRY:

Then th' moon murmur'd, I feel hot, 'n fear a storm is brewing,

DARRY:

Down where the bees are hummin' an' the wild flowers gaily growing.

BARRY:

She talk'd so well of things so high, he started to reward her,

The moon ran in behind a cloud, for there was none to guard her.

I'll take that off, she said, you'd ruin the lace that's round the border,

DARRY:

Down where the bees are hummin' an' the wild flowers gaily growing.

BARRY:

White-featur'd 'n thin goodie-goodies rush around excited.

DARRY:

Down where the bees are hummin' an' the wild flowers gaily growing;

BARRY:

Proclaiming that the dignity of living has been blighted,

DARRY:

Down where the bees are hummin' an' the wild flowers gaily growing.

BARRY:

But when the light is soft 'n dim, discovery disarming,

The modest moon behind the clouds, young maidens, coy 'n charming,
Still cuddle men who cuddle them, 'n carry on alarming,

DARRY:

Down where the bees are hummin' an' the wild flowers gaily growing.

[*When the song has ended,* DARRY *cocks his ear and listens*]

BARRY: Shall we try it once more?

DARRY: Shush, shut up, can't you?

[DARRY *goes over to the door, opens it, and listens intently. There is heard the rattling whirr caused by the steady and regular movement of a mowing machine. The distant Town Hall clock strikes nine*]

DARRY: [*Hastily putting the mandolin away*]   I forgot. I'll have to get going.

BARRY: Get going at what?

DARRY: House-work. [*He begins to get into the overall left off by* LIZZIE]   I dared her, an' she left me to do the work of the house while she was mowing the meadow. If it isn't done when she comes back, then sweet goodbye to the status I had in the home. [*He finds it difficult to get the overall on*]   Dih dih dih, where's the back 'n where's the front, 'n which is which is the bottom 'n which is the top?

BARRY: Take it quietly, take it quietly, Darry.

DARRY: [*Resentfully*]   Take it quietly? An' the time galloping by? I can't stand up on a chair 'n say to the sun, stand thou still there, over the meadow th' missus is mowing, can I?

BARRY: I know damn well you can't, but you're not going to expedite matters by rushing around in a hurry.

DARRY: [*He has struggled into the overall*]   Expedite matters! It doesn't seem to strike you that when you do things quickly, things are quickly done. Expedite matters! I suppose loitering to look at you lying on the broad of your back, jiggling your legs about, was one way of expediting matters; an' listening to you plucking curious sounds out of a mandolin, an' singing a questionable song, was another way of expediting matters?

BARRY: You pioneered me into doing two of them yourself.

DARRY: [*Busy with the pot on the fire*]   I pioneered you into doing them! Barry Derrill, there's such a thing in the world as a libel. You came strutting in with a mandolin under your arm, didn't you?

BARRY: I did, but——

DARRY: An' you sang your song.

BARRY: Yes, but——

DARRY: When you waltz'd in, I was doing callisthenics, wasn't I?

BARRY: I know you were; but all the same——

DARRY: An' you flung yourself down on the floor, and got yourself into a tangle trying to do them too, didn't you?

BARRY: Hold on a second——

DARRY: Now, I can't carry the conversation into a debate, for I have to get going. So if you can't give a hand, go, 'n let me do the things that have to be done, in an orderly 'n quiet way.

BARRY: 'Course I'll give a hand—only waiting to be asked.

DARRY: [*Looking at the clock, suddenly*] Is the clock stopped?

BARRY: [*Taking up clock and putting it close to his ear*] There's no ticking, 'n it's hours slow.

DARRY: Lizzie again! Forgot to wind it. Give the key a few turns, Barry, an' put the hands on to half-past nine.

[BARRY *starts to wind the clock.* DARRY *goes over to table, gets a basin of water, begins to wash the delf, humming to himself the air of the song, 'Down where the bees are humming'.* BARRY *winds and winds away, but no sign is given of a tightening of the spring inside. He looks puzzled, winds again, and is about to silently put the clock back where he found it, when* DARRY *turns and looks at him questioningly*]

DARRY: You've broken the damn thing, have you?

BARRY: I didn't touch it.

DARRY: Didn't touch it? Amn't I after looking at you twisting an' tearing at it for nearly an hour? [*He comes over to* BARRY] Show me that. [*He takes the clock from* BARRY *and opens the back, and the spring darts out*] Didn't touch it. Oh, for God's sake be more careful when you're handling things in this house! Dih dih dih. [*He pushes the spring back, and slaps the clock down on the dresser*] You must have the hands of a gorilla, man. Here, come over 'n wipe while I wash.

[*A slight pause while the two of them work at the delf.* DARRY *anxiously watches* BARRY, *who, being very near-sighted, holds everything he wipes close up to his spectacles*]

DARRY: [*Suddenly*] Look out, look out, there—you're not leaving that jug on the table at all; you're depositing it in the air, man!

BARRY: [*Peering down at the table*] Am I? Don't be afraid, I won't let anything drop.

DARRY: [*Humming the song*] Dum dah de de dum da dee dee dum dah dee dee dee dah ah dum.

BARRY: [*Swinging his arm to the tune*] Down where the bees are hummin' an' the wild flowers gaily growing.

DARRY: Fine swing, you know. Dum dah dee dee dum dah dee dee dum dah dee dee dee dah ah dum.

BARRY: [*Swinging his arm*]   Down where the bees are hummin'——
[BARRY'*s arm sends the jug flying off the table on to the floor*]

DARRY: [*Yelling*]   You snaky-arm'd candle-power-ey'd elephant, look at what you're after doing!

BARRY: [*Heatedly*]   It's only a tiny jug, anyhow, 'n you can hardly see the pieces on the floor!

DARRY: [*Just as heatedly*]   An' if I let you do much more, they would soon be big enough to bury us! Sit down, sit down in the corner there; do nothing, say nothing, an', if I could, I'd put a safety curtain round you. For God's sake, touch nothing while I run out an' give the spuds to the pig.

[DARRY *dashes over to the fire, whips the pot off, and runs out. He leaves the door open, and again the rattling whirr of a mowing machine can be heard.* BARRY *sits dejectedly in a corner. After a few moments a bump is heard outside, followed by a yell from* DARRY, *who, a second later, comes rushing madly in, a bloody handkerchief pressed to his nose. He flings himself flat on the floor on his back, elevating his nose as much as possible*]

DARRY: Get me something cold to put down the back of my neck, quick!

BARRY: [*Frightened*]   What the hell did you do to yourself?

DARRY: I didn't bend low enough when I was going in, 'n I gave myself such a—oh, such a bang on my nose on the concrete. Get something cold, man, to shove down the back of my neck 'n stop the bleeding!

BARRY: Keep the nose sticking up in the air as high as you can. I don't know where to get something cold to shove down the back of your neck. I knew this rushing round wouldn't expedite matters.

DARRY: [*With a moan of resentment as he hears 'expedite matters'*]   Oh, pull yourself together, man, 'n remember we're in the middle of an emergency.

BARRY: A little block of ice, now, would come in handy.

DARRY: A little—oh, a little block of ice! An' will you tell us where you're going to get a little block of ice? An', even if we had one, how could you fasten it down the back of my neck? Eh? Can't you answer—where are you going to get a block of ice?

BARRY: How the hell do I know where I'm going to get it?

DARRY: D'ye expect me to keep lying here till the winter comes?

[*During this dialogue* BARRY *is moving round the room aimlessly, peering into drawers, rattling the delf on the dresser with his nose as he looks along the shelves*]

DARRY: [*As he hears the crockery rattling*]   Mind, mind, or you'll break something. I must be losing a lot of blood, Barry, an' I won't be able to keep my nose sticking up in the air much longer. Can't you find anything?

BARRY: I can see nothing.

DARRY: Run upstairs 'n get the key of the big shed that's hanging on the wall, somewhere over the mantelpiece at the far end of the room. Go quick, man!

[BARRY *runs upstairs, goes into room, comes out again, and looks down at* DARRY]

DARRY: [*Up to him*]   Did you get it?

BARRY: Where's the switch? It's as dark as pitch in there.

[DARRY, *with a moan of exasperation, sits up, but immediately plunges down on his back again*]

DARRY: Starts pumping out again the minute I sit up. [*To* BARRY]   There's no switch in that room. We can't have a switch in every corner of the room just to suit you! You've only got to move down the centre of the room till you come to the fireplace; then brush your hand over the mantelpiece, along the wall, till you feel the key hanging there.

[BARRY *goes back into the room. After a few seconds' silence, there is a crash of falling crockery.* DARRY, *after a second of silent consternation, sits up with a jerk, but immediately plunges down on his back again*]

DARRY: [*Sinking supine on the floor*]   What has he done now; oh, what has he done now? [*Shouting up to* BARRY]   Eh, you up there—what have you done now?

BARRY: [*Sticking his head out of the door above*]   Nothing much—the washhand-stand fell over.

DARRY: [*Angrily*]   Nothing much. It sounded a hell of a lot, then. You're the kind of man if you're not chained up, 'll pull everything in the house asundher! Come down, come down, 'n stop down, or that delicate little hand of yours 'll smash everything in the house!

BARRY: My eyes are used to the darkness, now, 'n I can see. I'll get the key for you.

[*He goes back into the room, leaving* DARRY *speechless. After a few seconds, he comes out of the room in a sweat of fright and anger, one hand tightly clasped over the other. He rushes down the stairs, and begins to pull the things out of the chest of drawers, every other moment leaving off to clasp one hand over the other*]

BARRY: [*Frantically*]   Get your own key, get your own key. Half slaughtering myself for your sake! Why don't you keep your razor-blades in a safe place, an' not leave them scattered about in heaps all over the mantelpiece? Where is there a bit of old rag till I bind up my wounds? Get your own key yourself, I'm tellin' you.

DARRY: Amn't I nicely handicapped, wanting help an' having only the help of a half-blind man?

BARRY: D'ye know I'm nearly after mowing my fingers off with your blasted razor-blades? [*Coming near to* DARRY, *with a handkerchief in his hand, and showing the injured fingers to him*] Look at them, uh, look at them—one looks as if only a thin thread of flesh was keeping it on. How am I going to play the mandolin now?

DARRY: You'd play it better if all your fingers were off.

BARRY: [*Keeping the wounded hand in the air, and holding out the handkerchief to* DARRY *with the other*] Here, get a grip of this 'n help me to bind up me wounds.

[BARRY *kneels down beside the prostrate* DARRY, *who takes the handkerchief and proceeds to tie it round* BARRY'S *wounded fingers*]

DARRY: [*Keeping his nose well up in the air*] You give that an unexpected honour, if you call that a wound!

[DARRY *ties the handkerchief round* BARRY's *hand, who stands looking at it*]

BARRY: [*Reflectively*] Won't be able to do much for you with it now.

DARRY: It'll limit your capacity for breakin' things.

[*A pause*]

DARRY: Slip out, Barry, old son, 'n see if the heifer's safe on the bank beside the house.

[BARRY *goes outside the door and stands looking up towards the top of the house. The light has been fading, and it is getting dark. Again can be heard the whirr of the mowing machine, and the Town Hall clock strikes ten*]

BARRY: I think I can hear her croppin' the grass all right, but it doesn't seem wise to leave her there 'n the dusk fallin'.

DARRY: [*Testily*] I can't do anything till this bleeding stops, can I?

BARRY: The spuds are all scattered about here where you let them fall when you were runnin' in.

DARRY: [*Moaning*] 'N can't you get the broom 'n sweep them up into a corner, 'n not be trampling them into the ground; you see the state I'm in!

[BARRY *gets the broom and starts to sweep outside the door*]

BARRY: [*In to* DARRY] How's it now?

DARRY: [*Cautiously sitting up*] It's nearly stopped now, but I'll have to go cautious.

[BARRY, *sweeping with one hand, manages to bring the broom-handle into contact with the window, and breaks a pane. A silent pause*]

BARRY: [*As if he didn't know*] What's that, what's that?

DARRY: [*In an agony of anger*] What's that, what's that? Can't you see, man, that you're after thrustin' the handle of the broom through one of the windows?

BARRY: [*Peering down at the hole in the window*]   That's curious, now, for I never felt the handle touchin' the window; but there's a hole in it, right enough.

DARRY: [*With angry mockery*]   No, you wouldn't feel it touchin' it, either. A hole in it—of course there's a hole in it! My God Almighty, I've a destroyin' angel in the house!

BARRY: Well, not much use of looking' at it now.

DARRY: [*Vehemently*]   Oh, come in, come in, come in, man. Didn't you hear the clock strikin' ten? I'll have to get goin' now.

[*He gets up gingerly, feeling his nose, and still keeping it at a high angle*]

BARRY: [*Introducing another subject*]   Hadn't you better stable the heifer before you do anything?

DARRY: [*Violently*]   Haven't I to clean out the cowhouse first before I stable her, man? With your exercisin', 'n your singin', 'n your great 'n godly gift of expeditin' matters, I haven't made a bit of headway! I hadn't a chance to give her the graze she needs, so let her get all she can on the bank at the back of the house.

BARRY: Supposing she wanders to the edge of the bank 'n tumbles off?

DARRY: I don't know what to do about that.

BARRY: Couldn't you tie her to something?

DARRY: [*Angrily*]   There's nothing to tie her to, man.

BARRY: What about putting a rope down the chimney 'n tying it to something in the room?

DARRY: [*After a few seconds' thought*]   That's a good idea, Barry. There's a rope outside, an' I'll sling one end round her neck, let the other end down the chimney, an' tie it to a chair. Wait here a second 'n get it when it comes down.

[DARRY *rushes out. After a few moments his voice is heard faintly from above calling,* 'Hello, hello!' BARRY, *who has his head a little up the chimney, the smoke making him cough, answers,* 'Righto, let her come.' *The rope comes down;* BARRY *catches the end and pulls it into the room.* DARRY *returns, and they tie the rope to a chair*]

BARRY: Put the chair at the far end of the room, an' if the heifer wanders too far, we'll see the chair moving across the room.

DARRY: [*With enthusiasm*]   Now you're beginnin' to use your brains at last, Barry, me boy. [*He shifts the chair to the far end of the room*]   Now we can get goin' 'n get everything shipshape before the missus toddles back. Let's put on the light and see what we're doin'.

[*He snaps down the switch, but no light comes into the bulb*]

DARRY: [*Annoyed*]   Dih dih dih—must be the meter again.
  [*He hurries into the lumber room, stepping over the rope*]
BARRY: [*Speaking in to* DARRY]   I wouldn't do much tamperin' with that.
DARRY: [*Inside room—emphatically*]   Oh, I know what I'm doin'.
  [DARRY *rushes out again, snaps down the switch, but no light comes*]
DARRY: [*Irritably*]   Must be the blasted bulb. [*He rushes to a drawer*]   There's a bulb here, somewhere, we've had for a long time, 'n never used. [*He takes one from the drawer*]   Here we are. [*He pulls a chair to the centre of the room, stands on it, takes off the old bulb, and gives it to* BARRY]   See if you can see anything wrong with it.
BARRY: [*Holding it to his nose*]   Can't see anything.
DARRY: Leave it down, leave it down.
BARRY: Sure the one you're fixing's the right voltage?
DARRY: [*Stopping to look at* BARRY]   Course it's the right voltage. Why wouldn't it be the right voltage?
BARRY: If it wasn't, it might fuse.
DARRY: Fuse? No fear of it fusing.
  [*He starts to work again*]
  [*The chair to which the rope is tied begins to move across the floor*]
BARRY: [*Startled*]   Look out, look out—the heifer's moving!
DARRY: Catch hold of it, catch hold of it, before she disappears up the chimney!
  [BARRY *catches the chair, but the strain is too much, and he is pulled along.* DARRY *jumps down off the chair, leaves the bulb on the table, catches hold of the rope, and helps* BARRY *to tug the chair back to the far end of the room*]
DARRY: You sit on the chair, 'n then she can't move without our knowledge.
  [BARRY *sits on the chair;* DARRY *mounts the chair again, and starts to fix the bulb. The chair begins to move with* BARRY *sitting on it*]
BARRY: [*Excitedly*]   Eh, quick again, get down, the heifer's movin'!
  [DARRY *jumps down again, and the two of them pull the chair back to its place*]
DARRY: The missus'll be back 'n nothin' done but damage.
  [*He gets up again and fixes the bulb; there is a flash, and the room is darker than ever*]
BARRY: [*Like a prophet*]   I warned you, Darry; I saw it comin'.
DARRY: [*Forcibly*]   What are you blatherin' about? We're no worse off than we were before we fixed it. There's a drum of oil in the lumber room, 'n if there's any left in it we can light the lamps. You light the one hangin' on the wall, while I see how we stand.

[*He runs into the lumber room.* BARRY *takes the lamp from the wall, removes the chimney, and tries to light the wick, but he can't see it, and holds the match anywhere but near the wick.* DARRY *comes out of cellar*]

DARRY: [*Jubilantly*]   Plenty of oil in it. Aw, you're not holding the match within a mile of the wick, man. Show it to me, show it to me.

[*He takes the match from* BARRY, *and lights the lamp*]

DARRY: Out with you now, 'n get one of the old lamps you'll find on one of the shelves to the right in the shed at the back of the yard.

BARRY: How'll I see?

DARRY: Strike a match 'n look. You'll see them staring at you. I'll take a canful of oil from the drum to put in it when you bring it back, 'n then we'll have lashin's of light.

BARRY: [*Going out by door*]   I know I won't be able to see.

[DARRY, *with a can that has a long snout on it, runs back into the lumber room.* BARRY *has left the door open, and the rattling whirr of the mowing machine can be heard again. There is a slight pause. Suddenly* DARRY *rushes out of the lumber room over to the open door*]

DARRY: [*Shouting madly*]   Barry, Barry, come here quick, man! I turned the key of the tap too much, 'n it slipped out of me hand into a heap of rubbish 'n I can't turn off the cock, 'n I can't find the key in the dark. Come quick, man, or there won't be a drop of oil left in the drum!

[*He rushes wildly back into the lumber room. Another slight pause. He rushes out again, with the drum in his arms, his thumb pressed to the tap outlet, and runs over to the door*]

DARRY: [*Calling madly*]   Eh, Barry, Barry, d'ye hear me callin' you, man? I won't be able to keep this oil in much longer. Have you fallen asleep, or what?

[*There is heard outside a rattle, followed by a crash of falling pots, tins, and tools; then a dead silence for a moment*]

DARRY: [*Staggering against the wall*]   Aw, Mother o' God, what's he after doin' now!

BARRY: [*Outside, in a loud voice of great distress*]   Darry, oh, Darry, I'm after nearly destroyin' meself! Where's the doorway?—I can't see!

DARRY: [*Going over and standing in the doorway*]   Here, here, man; no, to the left. [*As* BARRY *staggers in, dusty and frightened*]   What ruin are you after causin' now?

BARRY: [*Moaningly*]   I'm after gettin' an awful shock!

DARRY: [*Appealingly*]   Pull yourself together, for God's sake, man, 'n tell us what's happened.

BARRY: [*As he sinks down on a chair*]   The blasted lamps were on top of the top shelf; there was nothing to stand on; I had to climb upon the shelves, and climbing up, the shelves 'n all that was on them came down on top of me!

[DARRY *goes over and rests the drum in the sink, his hand still pressed over the outlet of the tap*]

DARRY: 'N why did you climb the shelves? What did you want to do that for? Couldn't you see, you sap, that they weren't fixed well in the wall? Why did you insist on climbing the shelves?

BARRY: I was just tryin' to expedite matters.

DARRY: [*With a wail*]   Tryin' to expedite matters. Oh, there'll be a nice panorama of ruin in front of Lizzie when she comes back!

BARRY: 'N me spectacles were sent flyin' when the shelves fell.

DARRY: 'N why didn't you grab them before they fell to the ground?

BARRY: [*Hotly*]   How could I grab them 'n they fallin', when I was fallin' too!

DARRY: [*Impatiently*]   Well, get the lamp then, 'n look for the lost key in the lumber room.

BARRY: 'N maybe let it fall, 'n set the house on·fire?

DARRY: [*Woefully*]   Oh, amn't I in a nice predic— The chair, the chair—the heifer's movin'!

[*The chair to which the rope is tied begins to move across the floor.* BARRY *catches it, tugs manfully, but he is carried on towards the fireplace*]

BARRY: [*Anxiously*]   Give us a hand, give us a hand, or I'll be up the chimney!

[DARRY *leaving the drum, runs over to* BARRY'S *side, grips the rope in front of* BARRY, *and, to get a safer hold, takes the rope off the chair and puts it round him under his arms. With great pulling, they get the rope a little back. The oil flows from the drum into the sink unnoticed*]

DARRY: [*Panting*]   Keep a strain, or we'll be up the chimney!

BARRY: How'm I goin' to get home tonight without me spectacles?

DARRY: [*Loudly*]   Keep a sthrain on her, man, keep a sthrain on her; we have to get this straightened out first, before we can brood over your spectacles!

BARRY: [*Suddenly noticing the oil drum*]   The oil, the oil!

[*He lets go of the rope, and runs over to the oil drum.* DARRY *disappears up the chimney*]

BARRY: [*Lifting the drum and shaking it*]   Not a drop left in it, not a single drop! What're we goin' to do n——

[*He turns and sees that* DARRY *has disappeared*]

LIZZIE: [*Speaking outside in a voice of horror*]   The heifer, the heifer!

DARRY: [*Calling out*]   Lizzie, Lizzie!

[LIZZIE *rushes in as* DARRY *falls down the chimney. He crawls out from the fireplace on his hands and knees, and halts there, exhausted and sooty*]

LIZZIE: [*Horrified*]   What in the Name of God has happened?

DARRY: [*To* LIZZIE]   Now you see the result of havin' your own way! Why the hell didn't you hold on to the rope when you took it off the heifer, so that I wouldn't come down with a bump?

LIZZIE: How'd I know you were hangin' on the other end?

DARRY: [*Indignantly*]   You didn't know—my God, woman, can you do nothin' right!

CURTAIN

SARTRE

The Trojan Women

(from Euripides)

Jean-Paul Sartre (born 1905) became the intellectual spokesman of a generation which saw the Second World War destroy all traditional values and beliefs. Five years of Nazi domination in Europe created a world in which old norms ceased to be either applicable or relevant. Hitler's so-called 'New Order' brought nothing but moral and intellectual darkness as the concomitants of the horrors of war. This situation was a decisive factor in Sartre's development as man and thinker.

Profoundly concerned with man's quest for freedom and identity in a world which denied both, he came ultimately to reject all traditional belief in the innate nature of a man created in the image of God, and in all forms of determinism. He rejected too, significantly in the twentieth century, Freud's belief in the controlling force of man's unconscious mind. For Sartre, none of these things has any true relevance to the situation in which man finds himself. Man's personality, his attitudes and values, are shaped by his experiences, and these are consequently subject to continual change. Only through the process of living itself does that personality become defined, both through its acceptance of responsibility, and through its relationship with others.

Sartre maintains that the essential nature of man is not something fundamental which is gradually revealed by experience: it is simply and only the product of that experience. 'Man is nothing else but what he makes of himself.' Every individual is free to choose the acts which he will perform. He alone is responsible, personally and individually, for every choice he makes. There is no scheme of values outside himself to which he can refer. If he thinks he finds one and accepts it, he is simply drifting along in a state of non-being, for those values which he passively accepts do nothing to define his individual personality. This state of existence is, in Sartre's definition, the 'absurd', but unlike Beckett, Ionesco or Arrabal, Sartre does not accept the absurd as the essential quality of the human condition. He insists that man has the possibility of imposing a meaning on a seemingly meaningless existence through a succession of consciously-chosen and self-determined acts. Only by exercising that freedom of choice, which is forced on him and which he cannot escape, does man 'exist' in any positive sense at all.

The plays of Classical Greece, which so often and so profoundly explore the moral dilemmas which confront men in search of freedom, have long provided the French dramatists with models upon which to base their own explorations of these themes. Sartre's contemporaries, Giradoux, Cocteau and Anouilh, all produced variations on Greek themes. Sartre's own first play, *The Flies*, produced in Paris in 1943 (and banned after a short run), was a reworking of the Orestes myth with an emphasis entirely on the question of moral freedom. *The Trojan Women*, dealing as it does with the freedom of choice or lack of it imposed on man by capricious gods, provides Sartre with a further dramatic analogy to the modern dilemma of mankind on all its levels.

In an article in *Bref*, the monthly journal of the Théâtre National Populaire, in February 1965, Sartre himself defined his interest in Euripides' play, and his purpose in reworking it in modern terms:

'When Euripides wrote *The Trojan Women*, these myths were already becoming suspect. Although it was too early to overthrow the old idols, the critical minds of the Athenians were already questioning them. . . . Though Euripides used the traditional form which superficially resembled that of his predecessors, he knew that his audience was critical of his content, and consequently his play carries overtones even when he is writing within the convention. Beckett and Ionesco are doing the same thing today, that is, using a convention to destroy a convention. . . . The Athenians probably reacted to *The Trojan Women* in a similar way to which contemporary audiences received *Waiting for Godot* or *The Bald-Headed Prima Donna*. That is, they were aware that they were listening to characters who had beliefs which they no longer held themselves. . . . I admit it was the subject of this play which first interested me. This is not surprising. The play had a precise political significance when it was first produced. It was an explicit condemnation of war in general, and of imperial expeditions in particular. We know today that war would trigger off an atomic war in which there would be neither victor nor vanquished. This play demonstrates this fact precisely: that war is a defeat to humanity. The Greeks destroy Troy but they receive no benefit from their victory. The gods punish their belligerence by making them perish themselves. The message is that men should avoid war. This is Cassandra's affirmation, which is taken so much for granted that it is unnecessary to state it. The effects are obvious enough. It is sufficient to leave the final statement to Poseidon: *Can't you see war will kill you, all of you?* . . . The play ends in total nihilism. But whereas the Greeks had to live with gods who were capricious, we, seeing their predicament from outside, realise that they were, in fact, rejected by the deities. I have tried to emphasise this, and Hecuba's final despair is the human reply to Poseidon's terrible ultimatum, in which the gods break finally with men and leave them to commune with their own death. This is the final note of tragedy.'

The problem which Sartre's play redefines is finally as insoluble as it is perennial.

CHARACTERS

POSEIDON	MENELAUS
PALLAS ATHENE	HELEN
HECUBA	LEADER OF THE CHORUS
TALTHYBIOS	THREE WOMEN
CASSANDRA	THE CHORUS
ANDROMEDA	

The Trojan Women
(from Euripides)

SCENE ONE

[POSEIDON *enters*]

POSEIDON: I, Poseidon, God of the Sea,
            Have abandoned my shoal of lively Neireides
                And risen from the deep
            To gaze upon this bonfire that was Troy.
                Many years ago with our own hands Phoebus and I
            Piled stone upon stone
                And built the walls of that proud city;
                    Since then,
            I have loved every stone of it.

[*Pause. He looks down at the ruins*]
                Nothing but ash will be left.
            Now there are no priests in the sacred groves:
                Only corpses.
            Our temples bleed. The Greeks laid waste to every one.
            On the very steps of the Altar to Zeus,
            King of all the Gods, and my own brother,
                They slit Priam's throat.

[*Pause*]
            These Grecian vandals, who sacked my city,
                Will carry their plunder off with them
                    To deck out their wives and children
                With the gold and jewels of Phrygia.
            Ten times the season for sowing the corn came round.
                Still the Greeks stayed there, watching,
                    growing old,
            Obstinately besieging the city.
                But now it's all over.
            Their ships are ready and only wait for the wind.
                It is not courage, but cunning which triumphs.
            Now the Trojans are dead: all of them
                But these are their women:
            Some to become officers' concubines; others mere
                slaves.
                That one over there with a fat belly,
            Is the poor Queen. She is weeping,

Grieving for her husband and her sons.
It is I who have been defeated;
For now who will serve or worship me
In all these streets of ash? Nobody.
Hera, my own sister-in-law, Goddess of Argos;
My niece, Pallas Athene, Goddess of Attica,
Combined their powers to destroy my
precious Phrygians:
To break my heart.
I am defeated: I give in.
What can I do with these ruins?
Farewell, noble city,
I shall never look upon your ramparts
Or gaze upon your glistening towers again.
My masterpiece is destroyed. Farewell!
But for Pallas Athene's spite
Proud Troy would stand here still.

SCENE TWO

[PALLAS *enters and goes up to him*]

PALLAS: Poseidon!

[*He turns, sees her and angrily goes to leave*]

No, stay
Most powerful God, whom we lesser deities worship,
Whom my own Father looks up to.

POSEIDON: When you're polite, Athene, you put me on my guard.

PALLAS: If I can put our undying hatred to one side
Will you listen to me?

POSEIDON: Why not?
It's always pleasant to have a family chat
Amongst mortal enemies.

PALLAS: Quite. Let's be civilised.
I've a proposition to make.
It's to our mutual interest: it concerns Troy.

POSEIDON: You can see yourself what's left of it.
It's a little late to have any regrets.

PALLAS: Don't worry. I'm not going to feign sorrow over
your city.
I decided to wipe it from the face of the earth.
And that's what I did.

[*Pause*]

              What I want to do is to punish those Greeks.

POSEIDON: The Greeks?

PALLAS: None other. Will you help me?

POSEIDON: But they're your allies. You've only just given them
        this victory.
      For the Goddess of Reason, aren't you being a
        trifle unreasonable?
    I've never known any other God switch so capriciously
        as you do
                from love to hate.

PALLAS: They have insulted me. Cassandra took refuge in
        my temple.
    Ajax dragged her out of it by her hair.
    And do you know not a single Greek
        Lay a hand on him or tried to prevent him from
          perpetrating
    This piece of sacrilegious profanity. Not one.
    And to top that, the temple dedicated to me now
        burns.

POSEIDON: Mine too.

PALLAS: Both of us desecrated.
        Will you help me?

  [POSEIDON *hesitates*]

        And comfort your Trojan dead?

POSEIDON: You are my niece. But you have done me a terrible
        injury:
      Don't imagine I shall forget it,
      Or omit to take my revenge.
      But I will help you.

PALLAS: We must bring about a catastrophic return journey.
      Zeus has promised me rain, hail and a hurricane
    And will hurl his shafts of lightning against their
        fragile fleet.
      You must gather up all your waves
    Into one great wall of water.
      And when it is as high as a mountain
      Fling it down upon them.
      As for those who reach the Straits of Euboea,
    Let the sea open up beneath them
      To suck them all down to oblivion.
    Let every single one drown;
      So long as Greece learns respect for me.

POSEIDON: It shall be done.

On the beaches of Mykonos, from Scyros to Lemnos,
   Against the reefs of Delos,
At the base of the promontory of Caphareus,
   My innumerable mouths shall vomit their corpses.
Return to Olympus, niece. Watch.
   When they start to cast off their ropes
Ask your father to send down his thunderbolts.

   [*They part, each to their side of the stage*]

SCENE THREE

   [HECUBA *is now seen for the first time. She is lying on the ground*]
HECUBA: [*Trying to get up*]
            Up you get, you poor old crone,
            Never mind your broken neck. You're on your knees
                  today: but tomorrow you may fall on your feet.
            Be patient, philosophical.
            Being sorry for yourself won't get you anywhere;
               It never does, it never did.
            Don't try to swim against the current,
               When destiny wants to destroy you: let it.
            But it's no use:

                        Not even my courage
            Can stand up to the flood of my grief
               In its full spate of sorrow.
            Now there is no sorrow in all the world
               Which is not my sorrow.
            I was a Queen: my husband, a King.
               I bore him fine sons.
            The Greeks cut them down, one by one.

            As for my husband, Priam,
            These same eyes that weep,
               Watched when they bled him on the steps of the
                  altar
            And saw his throat open like a mouth
               And his blood flower, then flow, over his golden
                  skin;
            While my daughters,
               Who were to be betrothed
            To the greatest kings of Asia,
            They have all been dragged off to Europe
               As chattels to bad masters.

O Troy,
Your full sails were bellowed with your own glory.
   They cracked in the sun and sagged.
It was only hot air that had filled them.

[*Pause*]

I talk too much, but I cannot remain silent.
   And silence cannot feel any more than words can.
Shall I then weep? I cannot: I have no tears left
     within me.
   I can only throw my body upon the indifferent
     ground
And let it mourn noiselessly
     rolling from side to side
     like an old hulk in a tempest.

[*She goes to throw herself down again, but stops*]
     No.
Misery is like loneliness in this:
   that both are left a voice with which to sing
That's where all song comes from,
    So I shall sing:

   O ships of Troy,
Did you know where you were going
   ten years ago
When your rowers sweated,
And your proud beams parted
   The passive seas of the World?
When every port was your harbour
Did you know then where you were heading?
   All your voyages had one destination;
You were going to seek that Grecian traitor,
Helen, wife to Menelaus,
   and bring her back to be
   Death to every Trojan.

   O ships of Troy,
From those white decks iron men once sprung,
For ten long years now you have lain
   Anchored in our own harbours.
But today you are to sail away again
Taking me, the Queen of your city, with you
   With shaven head and ravaged face

To be a servant at a servant's table.
Did you have to do all this for this:

> To bring a blood bath on my people,
> Plunge me and all these women into mourning,
> All because you wanted the glory once again
> > Of sailing across to Greece
> > To anchor where shame is fathomless?

[*She claps her hands*]
> > Get up there
> > You Trojan widows, Trojan virgins, all mated to the
> > > dead.
> > Have the guts to look down upon these smouldering
> > > ruins
> > > For the last time
> > > And articulate your grief.

LEADER OF THE CHORUS:
> > Your anguish, Hecuba, has ripped open our tent.
> > > Fear feeds at our breasts,
> > > > Claws at our hearts.
> > > What do you want us to do?

HECUBA: Look down at those ships in the bay.

A WOMAN: The Greeks are hoisting their sails.

ANOTHER WOMAN: I can see men carrying oars.

ALL: They are leaving.

LEADER: [*To others off-stage*]
> > Come out and see what's in store for you.
> > > The Greeks are getting ready to go home,
> > You poor wretches, come out here and see for your-
> > > selves.
> > > All of you!

HECUBA: No, no, not all of you.
> > Not Cassandra. Keep her inside. She's mad.
> > > At least spare me the last humiliation
> > > > Of letting the Greeks see me blush with shame.

A WOMAN: What will they do?
> > > Put us to the sword?

ANOTHER WOMAN: Abduct us, ravage us?

HECUBA: Think of the worst.
> > > It will be that.

[*To herself*]
> > A slave.
> > Whose? Where?
> > > In Argos? In Phthia?
> > On some island off the coast?
> > > A pitiful old woman

More dead than alive,
A useless hornet in a foreign hive,
Dragging out her last few days.
Or I will have to squat night and day
Outside somebody's door
at their beck and call;
As nurse to some Greek matron's brats;
Or worse, stuck in their kitchen baking bitter bread;
With nothing but rags to cover the ruins of my body
And only an earth floor to lie down upon?

[*Pause*]

And I was Queen of Troy.

A WOMAN: If I throw my shuttle from side to side for ever
It will never be on the looms of Ida again.

ANOTHER WOMAN: Every member of my family is dead. My home
burned to the ground.
Looking on these walls which smell so acrid
I know that I am seeing them for the last time.

LEADER: Be quiet.
Preserve your strength,
Worse misfortunes yet await you.

A WOMAN: Are there worse than these?

ANOTHER WOMAN: Yes. One night some drunken Greek
Will drag you to his filthy bed.

FIRST WOMAN: The thought of what my body may do
Makes me loathe each limb of it.

OTHER WOMAN: Uprooted.
To live away from here will be to live in hell.

ANOTHER WOMAN: I shall probably have to carry their slops.

ANOTHER WOMAN: Maybe I'll be a servant in Attica?
On the fertile plain of Penee,
At the foot of Mount Olympus.
They say life is good there,
Even for slaves.

FIRST WOMAN: Anything's better than to be taken to the banks of
the Eurotas.
There I'd see Helen triumphant
And have to obey Menelaus,
The butcher of Troy.

LEADER: Someone's coming.

OTHERS: Who is it?

LEADER: A Greek. Look how he runs.

He's coming to tell us what they're going to do
        with us.
This is the end. Though we haven't yet left our native
        land,
    We are foreign to it;
            As we are now things that belong to Greece,
    Their slaves. Even here, their slaves.

SCENE FOUR

[*Enter* TALTHYBIOS. *He speaks to* HECUBA]
TALTHYBIOS: You know who I am, noble lady,
            Talthybios, herald to the Greek Army.
        I often entered the gates of your city,
            To deliver messages from our generals.
        And I am now instructed to convey an edict to you.
HECUBA: The moment we feared has come.
TALTHYBIOS: I suppose it has: your future has been decided.
HECUBA: Where are we to go?
TALTHYBIOS: You are all to be separated.
        Each to different masters.
HECUBA: What masters?
        Are we all to be treated exactly alike?
            No exception made for anyone?
            Surely not?
TALTHYBIOS: No. Give me time: I will tell you.
HECUBA: I am waiting.
    [*Pause*]
            Cassandra?
TALTHYBIOS: You've guessed right.
            She is to be one of the lucky ones:
            Agamemnon himself wants your daughter.
HECUBA: As a servant to Clytemnestra?
            It is as I feared.
TALTHYBIOS: Not at all.
        The King of Kings wants her as his concubine.
HECUBA: His harlot?
TALTHYBIOS: He might even marry her. . . . in secret.
HECUBA: So.
            You know that she is already betrothed to the Sun,
                To him alone,
            And that the golden-headed god

insists she remains a virgin.

TALTHYBIOS: Of course. It's because her virginity can be guaran-
teed, she being a prophetess,
That she's so attractive to His Majesty.

HECUBA: Throw away the Temple keys, poor child;
Tear off your holy fillet
And cover your hair with ash.

TALTHYBIOS: Come now, worse things could happen to her
Than sharing a bed with a King.

HECUBA: And what have you done with my daughter Polyxena?

TALTHYBIOS: She serves Achilles.

HECUBA: But Achilles is dead.

TALTHYBIOS: She still serves him.

HECUBA: What strange customs you Greeks have.
To think that I gave her life
For her to spend it in a tomb.

TALTHYBIOS: She's one of the lucky ones, I can tell you.
Even Cassandra will often wish she was with her.

HECUBA: Why?

TALTHYBIOS: She has found peace there.

HECUBA: Is she alive? Can she still see the sky
Or the stars at night?
Tell me.
Your look of shame's your answer.

TALTHYBIOS: We have given her shelter.

HECUBA: Shelter from what?

TALTHYBIOS: The World.

HECUBA: True.

[*Pause*]

And Andromeda?

TALTHYBIOS: Well, of course, being Hector's wife,
She was considered something special
And goes to Achilles' son.

HECUBA: And what of me? Broken with age,
Unable to walk without this stick.
What work can I do?
Who could possibly want me?

TALTHYBIOS: Ulysses. A slave in his household.

HECUBA: No. No. Anybody but him.
I spit on that dog.
On that double tongued monster
Who breathes hatred and discord
Wherever he finds friendship.

Ulysses! O Women of Troy,
Now weep for me, your Queen
in misery alone.

CHORUS: And what about us?
What is to become of us?

TALTHYBIOS: How should I know?
It's not my business.
The small fry will be sorted out in lots.

[*To the* GUARDS]

Go and fetch Cassandra.
Agamemnon wants her within the hour.
What's that? The tent's all red.
Quick, stop any Trojan women
From burning themselves alive.
I can understand that a free people
Don't easily knuckle under to a catastrophe like this,
But I don't want any embarrassing suicides on my
hands.
Do you understand?
And certainly no human torches.
That might be a way out for them
But it would be a bore to me.

HECUBA: It isn't a fire there at all.
It's Cassandra.
She's mad.

SCENE FIVE

[*Enter* CASSANDRA]

CASSANDRA: May this flame,
This gentle flame,
Rise slowly, dance fiercely,
Round this torch of me,
And lift its impetuous pride
Against the thighs of night
And stand up straight within the supple air.
May Hymen bless the union that it makes
And grant that I, who was a virgin of the sun,
Shall its full quietus make, as I lie beside the King.

[*To* HECUBA]

Hold this torch, Mother,
Lead the cortege.

What's wrong? Why are you crying?
> Because of my father, because of my brothers?
It is too late to grieve for them
>> For I am to be married,
>>> Your tears should be of joy, of joy!
>>>> Take it.
[*She holds out the torch to* HECUBA]
>> You refuse? Very well,
>>> My own hands shall coax and carry this flame
>>>> To Hymen's couch
>>> Where a Greek is to take me.
> For even if the Queen of the Night
Set alight to all her stars,
>> And the entrails of the hemisphere debowelled
>>> burned in their orbits
I would not have light enough:
Darkness would mark my way
>> As I walked towards that bed
>>> Where I am to be joined to the enemy.

So may this flame rise higher and higher
>>> till it licks the sky,
For this is the day my life has grown to.
>> Now Phoebus, God that is my God,
>> Conduct this choir that is my choir,
>> And you, my Mother, dance;
>> Join in this dance for her who was your daughter.
> Oh please, Mother, to please me. . . .
>> And why are these Women of Troy
Not dressed for a carnival and singing hilariously?
Come, now all together, after me:
>> Oh woe, woe, woe.

LEADER OF THE CHORUS
> [*To* HECUBA]
>> Hold her back, Your Majesty,
>> Hold on to her,
>>> She doesn't know what she's doing
>>> And might even jump straight into his bed.

HECUBA: Give me that torch, child,
You're not holding it upright.

CHORUS: Her ecstasy is all despair,
> Misery has not made her sane.

CASSANDRA: They think that I'm mad.

Listen, Mother, I tell you
You should rejoice at this betrothal.
And if you see me
suddenly timid,
I want you to thrust me into Agamemnon's arms
and let him carry me off to Argos.
For once there, I will turn our marriage bed into his
tomb.
Helen had a thousand thousand Greeks killed beneath
our walls.
But I shall do even worse to them.
Cassandra will be their doom.
Through me, and because of me,
Their King, their great King, shall perish.
By my sacrifice their Royal house shall fall.
And I shall destroy his people
As he has destroyed our own.
So now is not the time to weep
Unless tears of joy,
So laugh as the wind laughs;
Let there be a gale of laughter;
For I swear my father and my brothers
will be revenged.

HECUBA: How? By you?
CASSANDRA: By me.
HECUBA: My child, you will be a slave, helpless . . .
How can you . . . ?
CASSANDRA: With an axe.
There, right in the skull.
I'm not saying it will be I who strikes the blow,
But I guarantee this King of Kings will bleed all
the same.
Oh, how he'll bleed!

[*Joyfully*]

As for me, they'll cut my throat.

[*Pause*]

A long time later, the son will kill his own Mother
And flee—dogs at his heels.
That will be the end of the House of Atreus.
Nobody will ever fear them again.

CHORUS: Don't, Cassandra.
You are embarrassing us,
And you are making your Mother feel ashamed.

Not in front of the Greeks, we beg you . . .
   Don't let our conquerors
Hear your prophecies
And smile at your distraction.

CASSANDRA: Why should I be silent?
   I speak only of what the Sun has told me.
      I could tell you more
         But it is too horrible.
   You are right. I will say no more.

[*To* HECUBA]

      Don't cry.
   The Greeks are victorious. But what now?
      What happens to them?
   I will tell you:
      they will be beaten, they will be humiliated:
   Some will fall outside Troy, others on the plains.
      They will perish in their thousands,
   Not in defence of a city on their native land
      As our men did:
      They will die for nothing.
   Few of them will ever see their homes again,
      They will not even be buried;
   Nobody will say a prayer over them;
      Trojan earth will digest their flesh
   And their wives will never find their bones.
      These wretches are all recruits,
         a slaughtered but unburied army.
         The vultures wait,
   And oblivion awaits them.
      Not a trace of these conquerors will remain;
         Not even their shadow.
      Except for a handful
         who will crawl back to Greece
      Only to find themselves unwanted and unwelcome.
   Apollo himself has told me
      How Clytemnestra has behaved in Agamemnon's
         absence.
      But I won't repeat it.
   And all this, for what?
      Ten years to seek out one adulteress;
   And their victory will be to find
      Their own wives have been faithless to them—
   And every man's a cuckold!

[*To* TALTHYBIOS]

This is what you call winning the war.
  True, we have lost it;
  But not our honour.
We have fallen on our own soil
Defending our own city.
Gentle hands waited to nurse our wounds,
And watching eyes waited to weep
  When we could bleed no more.
  When our King fell
    Troy itself was his widow.

[*To* HECUBA]

You should be grateful to these Greeks.
  They even turned Hector
Who was a modest gentle man
  Into an immortal legend of courage.
  We who defended our native land are glorified,
But those who conquered us shall be cursed.
  They started this filthy war:
They will die as stupidly as they lived.

[*To the* TROJAN WOMEN]

Lift up your heads: be proud,
  Leave your revenge to me;
He who embraces me will be destroyed by me.

A WOMAN: I wish I could believe you;
I wish I could laugh
  And be as crazily defiant as you are.
    But look at us,
  Take a look at yourself.
All your singing and spitting won't get you anywhere.
  It's all words,
    impotent words.

TALTHYBIOS: And they'd prove rather expensive
If we didn't know she was insane.

[*Aside*]

The more I see of the intimate lives of the great
  The more I realise they're as petty and perverse as
    the next man.
  As for the most mighty King of Argos
Who has taken it into his head
  to desire this creature who's not right in hers,
All I can say is: a poor devil like me
  Wouldn't want her for all the gold in all the World.

But there it is:
So come on, my pretty, follow us.
Let's get going.
You heard them: words won't help you now.

[*To* HECUBA]

I'll come back for you
Immediately Ulysses sends for you.
You won't find it so bad with him,
As servant to Penelope.
People speak rather well of her.

CASSANDRA: Servant? There's only one servant here
And that: you,
You insolent and obsequious lout
With the manners of a farm hand.
You don't know what you're talking about.
My Mother won't be going to Ithaca.
Apollo has assured me
She will die here, in Troy.

TALTHYBIOS: Not if I have anything to do with it, she won't.
Her suicide would finish me.

CASSANDRA: Who said anything about suicide?

TALTHYBIOS: How else?

CASSANDRA: You'd like to know, wouldn't you?
But I shan't tell you.
As for Ulysses and all his double talk,
That man doesn't know what he's in for.
He's got another ten years,
Another ten years of mud and blood,
before he sees Ithaca again.
Oh yes, I know everything's ready and he's about to
set sail,
But the end is often only another beginning.
The giant flesh-eating Cyclops
squats on his rock,
his mouth watering, waiting for him.
So does Circe who turns men into pigs;
Not to mention Scylla and Charybdis
who lick their lips at a smell of a shipwreck.
I tell you the only place Ulysses is going to is Hell.
We know a few who are waiting for him there.

[*To the* WOMEN]

I can assure you Ulysses will suffer.
Whatever your misfortunes are,

He will envy them.

[*She looks into the distance*]

That's it. When he eventually climbs out of Hades
And lands on his own island
He finds that it too has been conquered.

[*She emerges from her trance*]

But what's Ulysses to me?

[*To* TALTHYBIOS]

Well, what are we waiting for?
I'm impatient to be joined to my betrothed:
for better or worse.
No, just the worst.
So toll the wedding bells!
Our marriage shall be a cortege down the road to Hell
And this generalissimo,
this King of Kings,
Who wants to embrace the daughter of the Sun
Will never see the light again.
Endless night will devour you,
And your body will be chucked over a cliff.
Toll the wedding bells!
For our broken bodies will be naked together
And vultures alone will be satisfied;
Their beaks will be intimate with my breast;
Their claws shall caress your manhood.
Here I'll tear the veil of my virginity,
Of prophecy,
While my body is still unravished.
May the gentle breeze
waft it to the true God of Love:
The Sun, the Sun.
Now which is my boat? Where do I embark?
Since I am death,
See that a black flag
Flies at the mast of the ship which carries me.
Goodbye, Mother,
Be calm; you're going to die soon.
Father, I am coming,
I am coming to join you in your grave;
I won't keep you waiting,
I am coming to you at the head of a hideous cortege
Made up of the entire house of Atrides
Who slaughtered you.

Toll the wedding bells!

[*She goes off with the* SOLDIERS]

Dong! Dong!

Toll the wedding bells!

[HECUBA *faints*]

LEADER OF THE CHORUS:

Quick, Hecuba's collapsed.

Don't stand there. Lift her gently:

She's still our Queen.

[*They do so*]

HECUBA: I did not seek your concern

And I do not thank you for it.

What I wanted was to embrace the earth,

to yield myself into its blind unconsciousness.

For you see, we are all blind too;

We can do nothing but submit.

But unhappily, though we are blind,

we alone are conscious.

CHORUS: Oh Royal Lady,

Pray to the Gods.

HECUBA: [*Savagely*]

No. They are allies

Not to be relied upon.

Let us be silent.

CHORUS: Silence is something we fear.

HECUBA: Then stop complaining.

Better, think when you were last happy.

CHORUS: [*Alternating verses*]

That was yesterday.

It was only yesterday

that we were happy.

That was the same day Troy fell.

In the morning, we saw from the ramparts

That the beach was deserted

And their fleet had left our bay;

There in the middle of the plain

Stood a great wooden horse on wheels,

A wooden horse with a golden harness.

The People of Troy, seeing this idol

From the rock of the citadel,

cried out: 'It is over. The siege is finished.

The Greeks are gone. Our suffering is at an end,

So hoist their wooden idol into our Acropolis

As an offering to Pallas Athene,
    Zeus' noble daughter, who has forgiven us.'
        Everyone was shouting and singing;
Strangers kissed in the streets;
Old men asked what all the excitement was about.
    'It's peace, it's peace,' we cried,
and lifted them off their feet.
    We tethered ropes round this idol to haul it to
        Athene's Temple.
Everyone lent a hand, some pulling, others pushing.
    It took all day, not till dusk was it there;
Then our victory songs and the sound of Lydian lutes
        enlivened the night.
That was yesterday.
    All the houses in the city were dark and empty;
Everybody was out in the streets: dancing with torches,
Singing; nobody slept, it was a night of carnival,
A carnival of peace.
    That was how Troy went down:
In riotous joy!
    And that was only yesterday.

LEADER OF THE CHORUS:
    Nothing is more deceptive than happiness.
    Joy is a cheat which covers up for the misery
        stalking behind the grin.
    At midnight we were still singing,
        then suddenly the whole city
        rang with one refrain:
            it was the cry
                of death.
    War was back again:
    Pallas had forgiven nothing.
The Greeks had leapt out of the idol
And were slaughtering our men and boys.
    That was how our night of celebration ended
        with the dawn of death.

HECUBA: Troy wasn't conquered:
The Trojans weren't defeated.
    They were betrayed by a Goddess:
It's always a mistake to worship a woman.

LEADER OF THE CHORUS:
    Look, Your Majesty,
    A chariot is coming.

[HECUBA *doesn't move*]

A WOMAN: It's Andromeda, Hector's wife,
           carrying Astyanax in her arms.

   [*To* ANDROMEDA]
           Where are you taking him?

ANDROMEDA: To my master.

   [HECUBA *now turns, looks coldly at* ANDROMEDA, *and sees* ASTYANAX *who carries a small basket*]

HECUBA: Misery. Everywhere I look: misery.

ANDROMEDA: What are you crying about?
           It's my loss.

HECUBA: It's ours.

ANDROMEDA: No, mine.

HECUBA: You are all my children.

ANDROMEDA: Were.

HECUBA: I mourn for all my sons.

ANDROMEDA: But I only for one, Hector.

HECUBA: I weep for our burning city.

ANDROMEDA: I weep for Hector's city.

HECUBA: For our royal home.

ANDROMEDA: Only for the house where I became a woman:
           Where I gave birth to Astyanax.

HECUBA: It's burning: it's burnt.
           Everything's flattened: a shambles of ash.

ANDROMEDA: You are to blame.
           It was you who gave birth to Paris:
              that damned adventurer.
           Didn't the Gods themselves, foreseeing his future,
              order you to smother him?
           You refused: it is we who are punished for that:
                 for your pride
              Which you hawked around as a Mother's love.
           It was this precious infant of yours
              Which smashed Troy like a toy;
              And now Pallas alone can laugh
           At the heap of corpses piled up at the foot of her statue,
              While these vultures encircle us;
              and we stand here as slaves.

HECUBA: [*Broken, her face in her hands*]
           If Priam
              could cry out from Hell
              He would shout: 'You lie, you lie.'

ANDROMEDA: If Hector could come back

He would save me. He would revenge me.

[*Then quietly but without gentleness*]

I have never liked you.
You have never liked me.
But you're an old woman:
I feel sorry for you.

[*Pause*]

Polyxena is dead.

HECUBA: Dead? What a coward I am.
That's what Talthybios was trying to tell me.
And I hadn't the courage to understand.
Dead. How?

ANDROMEDA: They cut her throat on Achilles' tomb.

[*Pause*]

I saw her body.
I covered her face with a black veil.

HECUBA: Slaughtered on a tomb:
Like a goat, or an ox.
What a terrible death.

ANDROMEDA: Why terrible?
She is dead. That's all.
Better off than I who live.

HECUBA: What do you know of death or life?
I tell you death is a nothingness;
however painful life is
it is better than death: it has hope.
I prefer life at its worst to death at its best.

ANDROMEDA: Your will to live's insane.
You know very well you've nothing to live for,
Your sons are all dead,
And your belly is too old to breed any more.
Your future is completely hopeless.
So much the better for you.
You can give in and sink in your circumstances
Rather than clinging on to a life that's finished
As far as you're concerned.
If you do that you won't suffer so much.
For death is a void,
A void that is eternal and peaceful.
Listen to me: It is the same for Polyxena now
As it was before she was born.
For now she is dead, she can't suffer any more,
and is unaware of the suffering she once
experienced:

her sheet is wiped clean again.
But I still suffer, and I still know I suffer:
   Life has more to scribble over me.
I was a good wife and devoted Mother;
   Some of us are. But as many of us know:
It doesn't matter how a woman behaves.
   The world thinks the worst of us,
And slanders us if we give it half a chance.
   I didn't give it that chance. I stayed at home,
   Where the gossips couldn't get at me.
It was no sacrifice: I was happy
   Devoting myself wholly to Hector.
But you see, old woman, my virtuous life
   has been my undoing,
And my reputation for being chaste recoils on me;
      for it is that
Which now makes Neoptolemus,
   the son of the man who murdered my husband,
Demand me for his bed.
   I am frightened. I am frightened
   And it is myself I fear.
For I do not want my memory of Hector to be erased.
   But I am a woman,
And a woman is only a woman.
   They say it takes just one night of pleasure to
      master her:
A woman is only an animal.
   That is why I am frightened.
Hector was the only man I ever knew;
   I loved his courage, his wisdom, and his gentle-
      ness,
The touch of his hands on my body.
And now the thought that this same body
May groan for joy when some other man lies upon it,
   Makes me want to tear it limb from limb.
Polyxena was lucky:
   She was murdered still a virgin.

[*To* HECUBA]

Liar. You say life is hope.
Look at me. I'm alive. What hope have I?
   None.
I know what life's going to write on me.

LEADER OF THE CHORUS: You are a Princess,
   But misfortune levels us.

By telling us of your fears
You make me aware of my own.

HECUBA: When the sea is rough
Sailors sail into it bravely;
But when there's a tempest,
They haul their canvasses down,
And let the waves drive them where they will.
I do that: I yield and I advise you to do the
same:
My child, Hector, is dead. Your tears won't bring
him back.
Forget him: devote the virtues which he loved to
your new husband.

ANDROMEDA: You disgusting old slut,
To think that Hector's own Mother
Should turn pimp.
You're nothing but a whoremonger.

HECUBA: Do what I say,
For Astyanax's sake.
He is the son of my son,
And the last of his race.
Do it for his sake,
So that he,
Or his son's son,
May one day refound this city,
And avenge us.

[*Enter* TALTHYBIOS]

What now?

TALTHYBIOS: [*Going to* ANDROMEDA]
Don't hate me.

ANDROMEDA: Why not?

TALTHYBIOS: I am only a messenger.
It is my distasteful duty
To tell you what my masters have decided.

ANDROMEDA: Come to the point.
Don't be afraid to speak.

TALTHYBIOS: Your son.

ANDROMEDA: Are they going to separate us?

TALTHYBIOS: In a way. Yes.

ANDROMEDA: We shan't have the same masters?

TALTHYBIOS: He won't have one at all.

ANDROMEDA: You're leaving him here?

TALTHYBIOS: I don't know how to tell you.

ANDROMEDA: Spare me your scruples,
        Get on with your job, lackey.

TALTHYBIOS: They're going to kill him.

   [*Pause. She clasps her child to her, staring at him. He continues quickly*]
        It was Ulysses who persuaded them.
           He urged the Greek Assembly
        Not to spare the life of the heir to the Trojan throne,
           because he might sometime become the focal point
           of rebellion.
           The Assembly accepted his resolution.

[*Pause*]
        So it's no use holding on to him like that.
           Give him to me.

[*She resists*]
        Come on now. Hand him over.
           There's nothing else you can do.
        Neither your city, nor your husband,
           can protect you now:
           neither exist any more.
        Don't you understand, we give the orders now?
           Do I have to tear him from you?
        Don't be silly. Bow to the inevitable,
           Accept it with dignity.

[*Pause*]
        For God's sake, isn't there anything
           that can make you hand that child over?
        Can't you see you won't gain anything
           By trying my patience
           Or making the soldiers angry?
         If you do that, they'll just leave him to the vultures.
        But if you hand over quietly,
           we might even let you bury him,
        and our generals will treat you with more considera-
        tion.

ANDROMEDA: [*To the* SOLDIERS]
        Don't you dare lay hands on him!
        I'll hand him over. Later.

[*They back away, watching her. She looks down at her child in silence. Then slowly lifts up its hands one at a time, examining the small fingers. She then holds one of its feet in her hands; then runs her forefinger over the line of the child's mouth and eyes as though she had never seen the child, or any child, before. The* SOLDIERS *approach her. She looks up. They stop. She walks towards them holding out the child*]

ANDROMEDA: Here you are, take it: kill it.
                    Hit it with an axe. Throw it on a fire:
                        It's yours.
                    I can't protect it: I could only give life to it.
                        What are you waiting for?
                        Take it.

[*The* SOLDIER *goes to lead the child off when* ASTYANAX *spills his basket of sea shells. The* SOLDIER *bends down to pick them up and places them in the basket, then leads the child off*]

TALTHYBIOS: [*To the* SOLDIERS]
                    Carry it to the ramparts.
                    Wait for me there.

(*To himself*]
                    All very distasteful. I feel quite sick.
                        That's the worst of war:
                    Those who give the orders
                        Seldom see the mess it makes
                            When you hold a child by the feet
                    And bash its head in against a wall.

HECUBA: That child was my son's son.
                    There goes our future, mine and yours.

[*She puts her hands over her eyes*]
                    What a blessing blindness would be.

[*Exit* OMNES *except* HECUBA *and* THE CHORUS. *It is now dawn*]

CHORUS: Once again
                    The gentle dawn illumines a burned-out city.
                        This is the second time in our history
                    The brazen dawn has revealed
                        a tangle of limbs in our gutters,
                    Rubble spewing over our streets.
                        This is the second time
                    The Greeks have liberated us.
                        The first time, it was many years ago.
                    They invaded us from Salamis.
                        They told us then that they were bringing
                    Greek culture and European enlightenment
                        to the backward people of Asia:
                        Our city burned with progress,
                    Our young men had their limbs
                        amputated by philosophy.
                    The Greeks always envied our harvests,
                        their soil was eroded, ours still fertile;
                    That was all there was to it, many years ago.

But that time, though they sacked our city,
   they did not lay waste to the countryside;
They went away
      leaving us with the strength to rebuild.
   Our Gods were merciful then.
      But now they have abandoned us.
Though we lift our hands to heaven and cry:
      Save us! Save us!

[*A pause*]

Nobody answers. Only Echo.
      This dawn is indifferent: our Gods are deaf.

[*They sink to the ground. Enter* MENELAUS *with* SOLDIERS]

MENELAUS: What a glorious morning!
      This is the day of all days.
   The day I've lived for;
      There that slut sits now
   Squatting in a hovel, a prisoner
      at my mercy; I have no mercy.
   Now is the moment I have lived for:
      when I caught up with her again,
   And could make her suffer
      as she made me suffer . . .
   You will have guessed that I'm King Menelaus,
      well known for his misfortunes.
   Some people at home criticise me:
      They say I started this terrible war
   Merely because of a woman.
      But that's not fair.
   It was because of a man.
      And that man was Paris,
   The swine whom I took into my palace
      and who ran off with my wife.
   That's why this war's been fought.
      And I'm grateful that the Gods
   have punished Paris for his perfidy:
      Neither her, nor his city, exist any more.
   And now it's this woman's turn:
      this woman whose name sticks in my throat;
   Whose name I've never spoken for years, ten years.
      I have two alternatives:
   Either to have her executed here
      Amongst the ruins of the city she chose for her
         home,

Or to take her back to Sparta
  and settle her account there.
I've decided to do precisely that:
  for by postponing her punishment, I increase it.
When she reaches Sparta
  The mothers and widows of the Greeks
Whose men fell here
  will lynch her, stone her to death;
That'll be her end.

[*To the* SOLDIERS]

  Get her.
  Drag her out by her hair.
    Make her grovel at my feet.
  Then I promise you we'll hoist sails
    and only wait for a wind.

HECUBA: At last.

[*Pause*]

  At last I can believe in you, Zeus.
      You,
        the unknown
        and the unknowable,
      You,
  Who seated at the centre of the earth
    can, at the same time,
  hold the world in your hands
    like a ball in space,
      at last you have my grudging belief.
  At any rate, I believe in your justice
  For by this, I see that you do punish the wicked.

MENELAUS: That's a strange sort of prayer.
           Who are you?

HECUBA: Hecuba, Queen of Troy.

MENELAUS: I didn't recognise you.

HECUBA: Are you really going to punish Helen?

MENELAUS: I gather from your prayer
           that you'd like to see her put to death?

HECUBA: Of course.

MENELAUS: So would I. So would I.

HECUBA: That's what I meant by saying Zeus was just.
             Do it. But when you do it,
               Don't look at her.

MENELAUS: Why not? it's ten years since I saw her.
             I want to see what those years
               have done to her too.

HECUBA: Nothing. You should know that.
Women like her keep their beauty
because life doesn't touch them.
They're indifferent to the misery they cause.
They age late and then suddenly.
Her eyes are still beautiful,
though death looks out of them;
Her skin is still smooth,
For her lips, men will still slaughter each other,
and cities burn.

[HELEN *comes out from the tent*]

Go now. Don't look at her.
You think your desire for her is dead.
She will rekindle it,
And you'll be in her clutches again.

MENELAUS: Nonsense.

[*He turns and looks at* HELEN]
[*Pause*]

Release her.

HELEN: You need not have used force
to have me brought to you.
The instant I saw you, I wanted to run to you.
For though you hate me, I still love you.
I have wanted you. I have waited for you.

[*Pause*]

Let me ask you one question:
I will never ask another:
What do you want to do to me?

MENELAUS: I?

HELEN: You.

MENELAUS: To kill you.

HELEN: If you, my love, want my death,
then I, my love,
desire my own death too.
But just let me explain.

MENELAUS: No. I don't want to hear your explanations.
You're going to die. That's all.

HELEN: Are you afraid to listen?

MENELAUS: Aren't you afraid to die?

HECUBA: It's too late now. I begged you not to look.
But you may just as well let her talk.
There's no risk there
Whatever she has to say. I have an answer to it.
And will stuff her lies down her throat,

So let her talk of your past;
It will give you the courage
to see that she has no future.

MENELAUS: You needn't worry. There's nothing she can say
that will have any effect on me.
But I'll let her talk, since you want me to.
She knows only too well
There's nothing she can say, or do,
that will have any effect on me.
She's already dead as far as I'm concerned.

HELEN: [*Placing herself in front of him*]
No, do not turn away.
Look at me.
Have the courage to look at me for the last time.
Look on every part, then know what it is you're
killing.
You hate me? I do not hate you.
If only you knew. . . . Yes,
There are some things you should know. . . .
Oh, I know the sort of things I've been accused of. . . .
But I've an explanation for each.
I don't know whether you'll believe me or not,
But let me speak and have the courage to listen.

[*Pause*]

Do you want to know who is really to blame
for all this misery?
She is. That old woman. She was the start of it all.
It was she who gave birth to Paris.
The Gods themselves were alarmed.
They foresaw that that scoundrel would ferment a
war—and what a war.
They ordered her to smother him.
Did she do it?
No. And King Priam was too weak to make her.
All of this stems from that;
That was the beginning of it all.
Paris was only twenty when three goddesses
competed for his favours.
Pallas herself offered him the whole of Greece
if he'd choose her.
And with her behind him
he'd have overrun it in no time.
And what was Hera's bribe?

    She offered him Asia Minor.
And the whole of Europe.
    But Cypris offered nothing.
Nothing except me. She merely described me.
    She won. Paris chose her for his Goddess,
Then worshipped me.
        You were lucky then.
For if he'd chosen either of the other two,
    he would have conquered Greece.
If it were not for this body,
    which your soldiers have so misused,
You yourself would be a subject of that barbarian.
    But your luck was my misfortune.
        That you might escape
    I became the victim: Cypris sacrificed me.
And my beauty, my beauty became my shame.

MENELAUS: You slut. Why did you go?

HELEN: Darling, it was you, not I, who left.
    You were a careless husband
When you went off to Crete
    and left me alone with your lecherous guest.

MENELAUS: You could have resisted.

HELEN: I, a mere mortal,
Resist the goddess, Aphrodite?
    Could you do that?
A pity you cannot punish her
    for what she did to me.
If you could, you'd be stronger than Zeus himself,
    For even the King of the Gods
Is as much her slave as everybody else is.
    Why did I go?
    That's a question I've often asked myself.
And the answer is always the same:
    It was not I who left;
   But somebody who was not me.
Aphrodite was an unseen guest in your palace,
    like an invisible shadow to Paris;
And as you know, Cypris had made a bargain with
        Paris
    to give me to him as long as he lived.
There was nothing I could do
    to break that odious but sacred tie.
But the moment Paris was dead, I was free.

Immediately I did everything, everything I could
To get back to you.
At night, I climbed up on the city walls,
Tied ropes together to carry me to the ground
    where I might run to you.
Your own guards can prove it:
    because they always caught me.
That's all I have to say: that's my story.
    I am the victim of circumstance;
Destiny's plaything: abducted;
    married against my will to a man I loathed;
    forced to live in a foreign city I despised.
All this I endured to save my country.
    My own chastity was my contribution;
And there is nothing more precious to a woman than
            that.
    Yet, in spite of this sacrifice,
    they are wanting to stone me to death.
I am hated by the Greeks, detested by the Trojans,
Alone in the world, understood by none.
    Now tell me this:
Do you think it is right to put me to death
When it was the Gods, not I, who sinned?
    If you don't, then take me where I belong:
In our bed, on your throne;
    To do less would be to insult the Gods
Who, for all their mistakes,
        do not err in justice.

HECUBA: I'm beginning to doubt it.
CHORUS: Don't let her get away with it, Your Majesty.
    This woman is dangerous.
    Puncture her eloquence with a few facts.
HECUBA: Very ingenuous.
You'd like us to believe that the three Goddesses
    were as vain as you are?
That they would trade their holy cities
    to corrupt a jury at a beauty contest?
Is it likely that Hera would give
    Argos sanctuary?
Or Athene would ever deliver Athens to the Trojans?
    They were merely teasing Paris.
By trying to suggest that the goddesses are vain too
    You do not diminish your own viciousness.

          As for all this about Aphrodite:
You make me laugh, if I could laugh.
     Though I must say I liked your bit about
               Aphrodite
Entering the Palace as a shadow to my son.
     Tell me why would she bother to do that
When she can control us like marionettes
     from the comfort and security of heaven?
If King Menelaus wants to know the truth,
     all he has to do is to remember
     how handsome my son Paris was.
Immediately this woman saw him, she wanted him.
     That's all there was to it.
I'm tired of hearing people
     blaming Aphrodite for lusts which are all their own.
Paris was very good looking. He stayed with you.
     He was a Prince of Asia:
She was also impressed by the golden ornaments he
               wore.
          Greed added to her lust,
She didn't rest till she'd satisfied both desires.

[*To* HELEN]

          You always had to make do with the second best
               didn't you?
     Sparta is a poor country. There, even the Queen has
          to be economical.
     And you wanted luxury:
          You wanted to be able to copulate all night
          and chuck bucketfuls of gold out of your windows
          during the day.
     So you ditched your husband for a man you lusted
     after and traded your shabby little kingdom in
          for the richest city in the whole of Asia.
               It was good business, wasn't it?
     Yet you try to make out you were carried off
          against your will.
     Will. Odd that nobody saw this abduction.
          Strange you didn't cry out.
     Or if you did nobody heard you.
     And when your own people declared war,
          Came here to fetch you, and besieged this city,
     How many tears of remorse did you shed
          when you saw piles of Greek bodies

In heaps against these walls? Not one.
When things were going well for them,
   you conveniently remembered
   Menelaus was your husband:
His name used to spring to your lips then
   to keep Paris up to scratch.
But when the Greeks suffered any reverse,
   you forgot your first husband's name again.
Always an opportunist:
   Always keeping your eye on the main chance,
Never on virtue, never on loyalty to either.
   And of course now the Greeks have won,
You come here with some cock and bull story
   about trying to tie ropes together to make your
      escape
   and that the guards witnessed these attempts of
      yours.
You bitch, you know damn well
   all these men have been butchered
      and this because of you.
Unfortunately for you, and for me, too:
   I'm still alive.
You have one witness and this my evidence:
    How many times did I come to you
   And beg you to leave my son
   and go home to Greece?
I pleaded with you to do that,
   knowing Paris would, in time, forget you
   and marry again.
If you had gone through those walls
   the war would have stopped instantly.
And didn't I offer, again and again,
To have you conducted secretly
   back to your own people?
But you never listened, did you, my beauty?
   You didn't like the idea
 Of quitting that palace where you strutted like a
   strumpet,
Where every man ogled you, including King Priam.
   Just look at yourself now
Decked out with Trojan jewels,
   Your vapid face thick with make-up.
The lot. And the man you're trying to seduce now

             Is your own husband.
             You should be throwing yourself at his feet,
                wearing rags, your wig cropped,
                cringing for forgiveness.
             Menelaus, be firm. Don't listen to her.
                There'll be no peace for Greece
             Till she's done away with.
                Give the order, make an example of her.

CHORUS: Your ancestors will curse you
                If you hesitate.
             Your country will reproach you
                if you are weak.
             Be strong, noble. Punish her.

MENELAUS: That is my intention.
             I am convinced she left Sparta
                Of her own free will.
             All this talk about Aphrodite
                Is entirely irrelevant.

  [*To* HELEN]

             You dishonoured me:
             You shall die.
                The army will stone you.
             You are lucky: you won't suffer for very long.
                We endured ten years.

HELEN: You are my husband.
             You are my King.
                I implore you to forgive me.
             I have done nothing. No, that's not true, my darling.
                I know that I have hurt you.
             But blame the Gods for that, not me.
                Forgive me, take me back!

HECUBA: Let me speak now, not for my sake,
                Or Troy's sake.
             But for my enemies: the Greeks who died.
                Do not betray them.
                Do not betray their children.

MENELAUS: Be quiet, old woman!

  [*Indicating* HELEN]

             That creature doesn't mean anything to me.

[*To the* SOLDIERS]

             Take her aboard my ship.

HECUBA: But only a minute ago
             You were going to have her killed immediately.

MENELAUS: I was angry then.
   I now realise my original decision was correct.
     It is better she should die in Greece.

HECUBA: Perhaps it is.
   But don't let her go on your boat.

MENELAUS: Why not?

HECUBA: Because once a man has loved,
    As you have loved,
   His love does not die,
     even when it seems to be dead.

MENELAUS: That's true.
   But she whom I loved, is no more.
    I never loved that
     Or if I did, it was not me.
   But I'll take your advice, old woman;
    maybe it is wise.
   She can go on some other ship,
    And when she reaches Greece
    the wretch will die as wretchedly as she deserves.
   I'll make an example of her:
    It's not easy to make women chaste
   But where inclination fails
    I'll make terror teach them.

   [He exits]

CHORUS: Do you believe he will kill her?

HECUBA: It's an even chance.

CHORUS: Look! Look at the coward.
    What a liar he is.
   There she goes now right onto his own ship,
   And he trailing behind her.
    Now the game's up.
   She'll bring him to heel
   And reign unpunished over Sparta.
    Nothing pays off like crime.

HECUBA: And I thought you were just, Zeus.
    I must be going mad.
   Nothing will now ever assuage
    the bitterness our dead must feel
   As they, in their invisible battalions,
     crowd the beach
      to watch that brazen hussy
      step onto that ship,
   Knowing they died for nothing.

CHORUS: Absolutely nothing.
Helen will see Sparta again.
There she will reign:
Nothing pays off like crime.
Zeus has deprived us of everything:
Our temples, our incensed altars;
Our city, our fertile fields, our harbours,
and you leave us with nothing, though we were
innocent;
while you allow Helen
To show her heels with Menelaus,
and reign over Sparta again
as if nothing had happened.
Nothing pays off like crime.
The men whom we loved,
Who fathered our children,
will haunt these blackened stones
With all the anguish of the unburied dead,
While we, their widows, wander
in far-off lands with loneliness as our companion,
growing old, growing ugly,
and some of us becoming whores;
While that most honourable lady
calls for her golden mirror again
and sits contemplating her own smug beauty.
That's what it will be.
Nothing pays off like crime!

HECUBA: A pleasant journey, Helen.
May you drop dead on it.
If there's a God anywhere amongst all these Gods,
May he grasp all his lightning like a dagger
and strike that ship with it.
May it catch fire, sink.
And you, Menelaus, you impotent old cuckold,
May you drown too.
I'd like the sea to swallow you both up
then spew your swollen bodies on some beach
where your compatriots could contemplate your
beauty:
skin mottled and putrid,
flesh slipping from the bone;
Then they could see:
If crime pays off so well.

[*Enter* TALTHYBIOS *carrying the body of* ASTYANAX]

CHORUS: Look, look, look;
   Here's the little corpse of Astyanax.
   They dropped him like a stone from a high tower.

TALTHYBIOS: Hecuba, all our ships have now put to sea,
     except one,
   It waits for you and the rest of the booty.
   Achilles' son has had to leave in a hurry;
    War has started again in his country.
   A usurper has seized his father's kingdom.

HECUBA: Ten years of it here.
   Now it starts up somewhere else again.
    Always war somewhere.
   Has his father lost his throne?
    Don't expect me to be sympathetic.
     And Andromeda?

TALTHYBIOS: He took her with him.
   Before she left, she went and knelt by Hector's
    tomb.
   I found it moving, very moving.
   Neoptolemus was compassionate enough
    to allow a sepulchre to be built.
    And look at this.

HECUBA: His shield. Hector's shield.

TALTHYBIOS: By custom, of course, it belongs
   to the son of his conqueror.
   But in this instance, he's waived that right;
    So we won't be taking it with us
   To hang in the palace at Phthia.
   We thought that it might distress Andromeda
    To see this relic of Hector's
   Hanging on the walls of her new bridal chamber.
   And we didn't want to upset her.
    That would have been cruel,
   And we Europeans are both civilised
    and sensitive.
   So you needn't bother to try to find planks
    to make a coffin for Astyanax,
   Here it is! He can rest on his father's shield.
    My instructions are
   To hand over the body to you
    since his mother has already left.
   Here, take it.

Perhaps you'll let me help you
Bury it?
As you see, I've already cleaned it up
Or tried to; there was a lot of blood.
Here will do, won't it?
I'll help you dig; it needn't be very deep.
As I say, our ship's waiting.
After ten years, I can hardly believe it.

HECUBA: Lay this shield
Upon the earth
it protected.
I loved him.
This ring is still polished
where it was rubbed by his arm.
And now this eye of brass,
which once turned back the sun,
Will lie where no light can look on it
As a coffin for his son.

[*She takes* ASTYANAX *in her arms*]
Bloody Greeks!
Drunk with power
yet frightened of a child.
With Hector dead, our army slaughtered
and our city a cinder
you were still frightened of a child.
If you feared him, you will soon fear one another:
Civil war will do to you
what you have done to us.
And when both Troy and Greece
have been levelled as war levels,
All that will remain
will be this little tomb
standing among these shattered columns.
On it, it shall bear this inscription:
'Here lies a child
murdered
because he frightened Greece.'

[*Over the body*]
Little one,
You will never grow to strength,
Or know that love
Which makes a man equal to a God.
Nor will you fall or fail

As men do, from weakness or from age;
　　But if men can be happy,
You could have been happy,
　　All life's possibilities
Were held in this tiny hand. . . .
I always said he had his father's hands.
Now that which moved is still,
　　　　forever still,
and the blood congeals on his battered skull.
　　　　What waste, waste, waste.

[*To the* WOMEN]

　　Go and find something
　　With which we can wrap his body.

[*Some* WOMEN *go into the tent.* HECUBA *lays the corpse on the shield*]

　　And to think I used to believe
　　　　in happiness.
　　I tell you destiny is drunk
　　　　and the Gods are blind, clumsy, deaf and in-
　　　　　　different.
　　A man's a fool if he thinks he's achieved happiness
　　　　Unless he's on his death bed.
　　Now I'll bind these wounds which will never heal.

[*They return*]

　　　　Did you find anything?

A WOMAN:　Only these rags.

HECUBA:　　Rags will do.
　　　　The dead are not particular.

[*The* SOLDIERS *place the body on the shield again and take it off.* HECUBA *watches this silently. Then she suddenly explodes with anger*]

　　You filthy Gods,
　　You always hated me.
　　　　And of all cities
　　　　　　Troy was the one city
　　　　　　You detested.
　　Why? Didn't we mumble prayers enough?
　　Make ritual and habitual sacrifice?
　　　　And all for what?
　　　　Today we suffer in hell.
　　And you smirk at us from heaven.
　　　　Keep your heaven!
　　　　Go on licking your lips
　　Over human misery.
　　　　But I tell you, this time

You omniscient immortals
　　have made one small mistake:
You should have destroyed us with an earthquake
　　if you wanted to sweep us out of the way.
If you'd done that
　　Nobody would have ever mentioned Troy again.
But as it is, we held out for ten years
　　against the whole of Greece,
And then were only beaten by a cheap trick.
　　We die, but we do not die.
Two thousand years from now,
　　our courage will still be talked about;
It was something real
　　like your injustice.
You have condemned me. Now I'll condemn you:
　　Soon all of you immortals
Will be as dead as we are!
　　Come on then, what are you waiting for?
Have you run out of thunderbolts?

[*Pause*]

　　　　　Filthy cowards!

LEADER OF THE CHORUS:
　　Don't. We beg you.
　　You'll bring down other misfortunes on us.
　　　　There's always something worse.
　　　　　Here it comes.
　　Look, they're setting light to the Acropolis.

[*Enter* TALTHYBIOS]

TALTHYBIOS: My orders were to destroy anything left standing.

[*To* AN OFFICER *of his suite*]
　　Burn Troy.
　　See that nothing remains.

[*To the* WOMEN]
　　When you hear a trumpet,
　　File down in an orderly fashion to the beach,
　　It will be the signal for you to leave.

[SOLDIERS *enter*]

[*To* HECUBA]
　　Ulysses has sent these men to fetch you.
　　Poor old woman, you'd better follow them.

HECUBA:　　Now is the mountain of my misfortune capped:
　　　　To be carried off
　　Leaving my Troy in flames.

I salute those flames.
The greatest city the world has ever seen:
    To be populated by rodents,
    Decorated by brambles.
I said the Gods were deaf.
    That was not true:
They are evil.
    It's a waste of time to ask them for help.
Better to rely on my legs.
    Come on, old bones, don't let me down.

[*She tries to walk away*]

TALTHYBIOS: Where's she off to? Stop her.
    She must have gone out of her mind.

HECUBA: Oh the pity of it. Poor Troy.

CHORUS: Troy is no more. But a memory. Our memory.

HECUBA: Oh the waste of it.
    So many hands,
    So many hours and hours of work.
    Its glory was that it was home.
        Now ash settles on what we were
    And smoke describes what we've become.

CHORUS: The pity of it.
    The waste of it.

HECUBA: [*Kneeling and beating the ground*]
    Oh earth, dear earth,
        Be merciful.
    Open up, take us into yourself.
    Don't let them part us from you.

CHORUS: What was that? That noise?

HECUBA: That groan was the sound
        A city makes when dying.
    The walls of Troy collapse. Stand firm.
        Now make them drag us off.
    No Trojan feet will ever walk
        willingly from Troy.

[*They are all dragged off. Black out*]

[POSEIDON *appears and looks down at the prisoners waiting on the beach*]

POSEIDON: Poor Hecuba,
    You shall not die among your enemies.
        I shall let you go on board
    Then later take you down
        Into my kingdom of the sea.

And I will raise up a rock to you
    near your native land
  So that my waves will break over you ceaselessly,
Repeating your innumerable sorrows.
[*He turns and calls*]
        Pallas! Pallas Athene!
      Let's get to work.
[*There is a flash of lightning. Then a pause*]
        Idiots!
  We'll make you pay for this.
  You stupid, bestial mortals
    Making war, burning cities,
    violating tombs and temples,
    torturing your enemies,
    bringing suffering on yourselves.
      Can't you see
      War
      Will kill you:
        All of you?

CURTAIN

PINTER

The Room

Harold Pinter (born 1930), though also considerably influenced by Beckett, has gone on to create a drama uniquely his own. Conscious of the radical change in man's situation since the War, he is disturbed by the total breakdown in communication, and so of meaningful relationships, between people. In his plays, people cease to be individuals and diminish instead into objects. In a world lacking moral or spiritual equilibrium, human action becomes progressively more motiveless, and the most common-place situations become gradually fraught with mystery, dread and menace.

Pinter exploits the fact that in everyday life conversations are often repetitious and rambling, full of illogicalities and irrelevancies, in order to expose the essential isolation of individuals and their total lack of any positive contact. Any sort of confrontation between two people, ending in some sort of revelation to one or both, is impossible in the world Pinter creates. His people use language, not to reveal themselves to others, but as a wall behind which they can hide, behind which they can maintain their isolation from one another. What they actually *say* is far less important than the preoccupations which lie behind their words; not only do those to whom they speak not listen, but the speakers themselves often appear uninterested in what they are saying. Though Pinter specialises in monologues, his emphasis is always on the unbalance of such conversations: his focus is as much on the listener as on the speaker.

Moreover, Pinter is not concerned with the background or off-stage lives of his characters. Their past histories or future conduct are of no importance to him. The only thing that matters is what happens in the space and time of the present, for only this represents a measurable reality, if reality can be measured at all. Once an action is in the past, there is no way of separating reality from illusion. Yet even the here and now becomes ambiguous. While all his characters perform actions, these do not help to define them as people. We know nothing about them except what we see and hear for ourselves, and even then we may be misled. Just as what they say of their past is often shown to be false, so their present statements are often self-contradictory and their actions inconsistent.

Pinter's plots are just as indefinite: we are often in doubt as to whether an event has taken place or not because we do not know whether or not to believe the characters. Pinter never explains the motives which lead a character to misrepresent reality; for him there are no absolutes. The impossibility of proving reality provides not only the major source of suspense in his plays, but their substance itself. It is essentially what they are 'about'. He is perpetually asking the question, 'What is reality?', and since life itself as we have come to know it today seldom, if ever, provides absolute answers, we cannot expect Pinter to do so. As he himself put it:

> 'The desire for verification is understandable, but cannot always be satisfied. There are no hard distinctions between what is real and what is unreal, nor between what is true and what false. The thing is not necessarily either true or false; it can be both true and false. The assumption that to verify what has happened and what is happening presents no problems, I take to be inaccurate.'

The Room, Pinter's first play, expresses in miniature all these preoccupations, which he later goes on to develop more fully. The room in which this play's action takes place occurs again and again in Pinter's subsequent work as a powerful symbol of his obsession with safety and security and the dangers of dispossession. Like the play itself, his later comments, made in two separate radio broadcasts, serve to define the problem with which he is wrestling while at the same time, inevitably, leaving it unsolved:

> 'Two people in a room—I am dealing a great deal of the time with this image of two people in a room. The curtain goes up on the stage, and I see it as a very potent question: What is going to happen to these two people in the room? Is someone going to

open the door and come in? . . . Obviously they are scared of what is outside the room. Outside the room there is a world bearing upon them which is frightening. I am sure it is frightening to you and me as well.'

CHARACTERS

BERT HUDD, *a man of fifty*
ROSE, *a woman of sixty*
MR KIDD, *an old man*
MR SANDS ⎫
⎬ *a young couple*
MRS SANDS ⎭
RILEY

The Room

Scene: A room in a large house. A door down right. A gas-fire down left.
A gas-stove and sink, up left. A window up centre. A table and chairs,
centre. A rocking chair, left centre. The foot of a double-bed protrudes
from alcove, up right.
BERT *is at the table, wearing a cap, a magazine propped in front of him.*
ROSE *is at the stove.*

ROSE: Here you are. This'll keep the cold out.
[*She places bacon and eggs on a plate, turns off the gas and takes the plate to the table*]
It's very cold out, I can tell you. It's murder.
[*She returns to the stove and pours water from the kettle into the teapot, turns off the gas and brings the teapot to the table, pours salt and sauce on the plate and cuts two slices of bread.* BERT *begins to eat*]
That's right. You eat that. You'll need it. You can feel it in here. Still, the room keeps warm. It's better than the basement, anyway.
[*She butters the bread*]
I don't know how they live down there. It's asking for trouble. Go on. Eat it up. It'll do you good.
[*She goes to the sink, wipes a cup and saucer and brings them to the table*]
If you want to go out you might as well have something inside you. Because you'll feel it when you get out.
[*She pours milk into the cup*]
Just now I looked out of the window. It was enough for me. There wasn't a soul about. Can you hear the wind?
[*She sits in the rocking-chair*]
I've never seen who it is. Who is it? Who lives down there? I'll have to ask. I mean, you might as well know, Bert. But whoever it is, it can't be too cosy.
[*Pause*]
I think it's changed hands since I was last there. I didn't see who moved in then. I mean the first time it was taken.
[*Pause*]
Anyway, I think they've gone now.
[*Pause*]
But I think someone else has gone in now. I wouldn't like to live

in that basement. Did you ever see the walls? They were running. This is all right for me. Go on, Bert. Have a bit more bread.

[*She goes to the table and cuts a slice of bread*]

I'll have some cocoa on when you come back.

[*She goes to the window and settles the curtain*]

No, this room's all right for me. I mean, you know where you are. When it's cold, for instance.

[*She goes to the table*]

What about the rasher? Was it all right? It was a good one, I know, but not as good as the last lot I got in. It's the weather.

[*She goes to the rocking-chair, and sits*]

Anyway, I haven't been out. I haven't been so well. I didn't feel up to it. Still, I'm much better today. I don't know about you though. I don't know whether you ought to go out. I mean, you shouldn't straight after you've been laid up. Still. Don't worry, Bert. You go. You won't be long.

[*She rocks*]

It's good you were up here, I can tell you. It's good you weren't down there, in the basement. That's no joke. Oh, I've left the tea. I've left the tea standing.

[*She goes to the table and pours tea into the cup*]

No, it's not bad. Nice weak tea. Lovely weak tea. Here you are. Drink it down. I'll wait for mine. Anyway, I'll have it a bit stronger.

[*She takes a plate to the sink and leaves it*]

Those walls would have finished you off. I don't know who lives down there now. Whoever it is, they're taking a big chance. Maybe they're foreigners.

[*She goes to the rocking-chair and sits*]

I'd have pulled you through.

[*Pause*]

There isn't room for two down there, anyway. I think there was one first, before he moved out. Maybe they've got two now.

[*She rocks*]

If they ever ask you, Bert, I'm quite happy where I am. We're quiet, we're all right. You're happy up here. It's not far up either, when you come in from outside. And we're not bothered. And nobody bothers us.

[*Pause*]

I don't know why you have to go out. Couldn't you run it down tomorrow? I could put the fire in later. You could sit by the fire. That's what you like, Bert, of an evening. It'll be dark in a minute as well, soon.

[*She rocks*]

It gets dark now.

[*She rises and pours out tea at the table*]

I made plenty. Go on.

[*She sits at table*]

You looked out today? It's got ice on the roads. Oh, I know you can drive. I'm not saying you can't drive. I mentioned to Mr Kidd this morning that you'd be doing a run today. I told him you hadn't been too grand, but I said, still, he's a marvellous driver. I wouldn't mind what time, where, nothing, Bert. You know how to drive. I told him.

[*She wraps her cardigan about her*]

But it's cold. It's really cold today, chilly. I'll have you some nice cocoa on for when you get back.

[*She rises, goes to the window, and looks out*]

It's quiet. Be coming on for dark. There's no one about.

[*She stands, looking*]

Wait a minute.

[*Pause*]

I wonder who that is.

[*Pause*]

No. I thought I saw someone.

[*Pause*]

No.

[*She drops the curtain*]

You know what though? It looks a bit better. It's not so windy. You'd better put on your thick jersey.

[*She goes to the rocking-chair, sits and rocks*]

This is a good room. You've got a chance in a place like this. I look after you, don't I, Bert? Like when they offered us the basement here I said no straight off. I knew that'd be no good. The ceiling right on top of you. No, you've got a window here, you can move yourself, you can come home at night, if you have to go out, you can do your job, you can come home, you're all right. And I'm here. You stand a chance.

[*Pause*]

I wonder who has got it now. I've never seen them, or heard of them. But I think someone's down there. Whoever's got it can keep it. That looked a good rasher, Bert. I'll have a cup of tea later. I like mine a bit stronger. You like yours weak.

[*A knock at the door. She stands*]

Who is it?

[*Pause*]

Hallo!

[*Knock repeated*]
Come in then.
[*Knock repeated*]
Who is it?
[*Pause. The door opens and* MR KIDD *comes in*]

MR KIDD: I knocked.

ROSE: I heard you.

MR KIDD: Eh?

ROSE: We heard you.

MR KIDD: Hallo, Mr Hudd, how are you, all right? I've been looking at the pipes.

ROSE: Are they all right?

MR KIDD: Eh?

ROSE: Sit down, Mr Kidd.

MR KIDD: No, that's all right. I just popped in, like, to see how things were going. Well, it's cosy in here isn't it?

ROSE: Oh, thank you, Mr Kidd.

MR KIDD: So I thought to myself, I'd better have a look at those pipes. In the circumstances. I only went to the corner, for a few necessary items. It's likely to snow. Very likely, in my opinion.

ROSE: Why don't you sit down, Mr Kidd?

MR KIDD: No, no, that's all right.

ROSE: Well, it's a shame you have to go out in this weather, Mr Kidd. Don't you have a help?

MR KIDD: Eh?

ROSE: I thought you had a woman to help.

MR KIDD: I haven't got any woman.

ROSE: I thought you had one when we first came.

MR KIDD: No women here.

ROSE: Maybe I was thinking of somewhere else.

MR KIDD: Plenty of women round the corner. Not here though. Oh no. Eh, have I seen that before?

ROSE: What?

MR KIDD: That.

ROSE: I don't know. Have you?

MR KIDD: I seem to have some remembrance.

ROSE: It's just an old rocking-chair.

MR KIDD: Was it here when you came?

ROSE: No, I brought it myself.

MR KIDD: I could swear blind I've seen that before.

ROSE: Perhaps you have.

MR KIDD: What?

ROSE: I say, perhaps you have.

MR KIDD: Yes, maybe I have.

ROSE: Take a seat, Mr Kidd.

MR KIDD: I wouldn't take an oath on it though.

[BERT *yawns and stretches, and continues looking at his magazine*]

No, I won't sit down, with Mr Hudd just having a bit of a rest after his tea. I've got to go and get mine going in a minute. You're going out then, Mr Hudd? I was just looking at your van. She's a very nice little van, that, I notice you wrap her up well for the cold. I don't blame you. Yes, I was hearing you go off, when was it, the other morning, yes. Very smooth. I can tell a good gear-change.

ROSE: I thought your bedroom was at the back, Mr Kidd.

MR KIDD: My bedroom?

ROSE: Wasn't it at the back? Not that I ever knew.

MR KIDD: I wasn't in my bedroom.

ROSE: Oh, well.

MR KIDD: I was up and about.

ROSE: I don't get up early in this weather. I can take my time. I take my time.

[*Pause*]

MR KIDD: This was my bedroom.

ROSE: This? When?

MR KIDD: When I lived here.

ROSE: I didn't know that.

MR KIDD: I will sit down for a few ticks. [*He sits in the armchair*]

ROSE: Well, I never knew that.

MR KIDD: Was this chair here when you came?

ROSE: Yes.

MR KIDD: I can't recollect this one.

[*Pause*]

ROSE: When was that then?

MR KIDD: Eh?

ROSE: When was this your bedroom?

MR KIDD: A good while back.

[*Pause*]

ROSE: I was telling Bert I was telling you how he could drive.

MR KIDD: Mr Hudd? Oh, Mr Hudd can drive all right. I've seen him bowl down the road all right. Oh yes.

ROSE: Well, Mr Kidd, I must say this is a very nice room. It's a very comfortable room.

MR KIDD: Best room in the house.

ROSE: It must get a bit damp downstairs.

MR KIDD: Not as bad as upstairs.

ROSE: What about downstairs?

MR KIDD: Eh?

ROSE: What about downstairs?

MR KIDD: What about it?

ROSE: Must get a bit damp.

MR KIDD: A bit. Not as bad as upstairs though.

ROSE: Why's that?

MR KIDD: The rain comes in.

[*Pause*]

ROSE: Anyone live up there?

MR KIDD: Up there? There was. Gone now.

ROSE: How many floors you got in this house?

MR KIDD: Floors. [*He laughs*]   Ah, we had a good few of them in the old days.

ROSE: How many have you got now?

MR KIDD: Well, to tell you the truth, I don't count them now.

ROSE: Oh.

MR KIDD: No, not now.

ROSE: It must be a bit of a job.

MR KIDD: Oh, I used to count them, once. Never got tired of it. I used to keep a tack on everything in this house. I had a lot to keep my eye on, then. I was able for it too. That was when my sister was alive. But I lost track a bit, after she died. She's been dead some time now, my sister. It was a good house then. She was a capable woman. Yes. Fine size of a woman too. I think she took after my mum. Yes, I think she took after my old mum, from what I can recollect. I think my mum was a Jewess. Yes, I wouldn't be surprised to learn that she was a Jewess. She didn't have many babies.

ROSE: What about your sister, Mr Kidd?

MR KIDD: What about her?

ROSE: Did she have any babies?

MR KIDD: Yes, she had a resemblance to my old mum, I think. Taller, of course.

ROSE: When did she die then, your sister?

MR KIDD: Yes, that's right, it was after she died that I must have stopped counting. She used to keep things in very good trim. And I gave her a helping hand. She was very grateful, right until her last. She always used to tell me how much she appreciated all the—little things—that I used to do for her. Then she copped it. I was her senior. Yes, I was her senior. She had a lovely boudoir. A beautiful boudoir.

ROSE: What did she die of?

MR KIDD: Who?

ROSE: Your sister.

[*Pause*]

MR KIDD: I've made ends meet.

[*Pause*]

ROSE: You full at the moment, Mr Kidd?

MR KIDD: Packed out.

ROSE: All sorts, I suppose?

MR KIDD: Oh yes, I make ends meet.

ROSE: We do, too, don't we, Bert?

[*Pause*]

Where's your bedroom now then, Mr Kidd?

MR KIDD: Me? I can take my pick. [*Rising*]   You'll be going out soon then, Mr Hudd? Well, be careful how you go. Those roads'll be no joke. Still, you know how to manipulate your van all right, don't you? Where you going? Far? Be long?

ROSE: He won't be long.

MR KIDD: No, of course not. Shouldn't take him long.

ROSE: No.

MR KIDD: Well then, I'll pop off. Have a good run, Mr Hudd. Mind how you go. It'll be dark soon too. But not for a good while yet. Arivederci.

[*He exits*]

ROSE: I don't believe he had a sister, ever.

[*She takes the plate and cup to the sink.* BERT *pushes his chair back and rises*]

All right. Wait a minute. Where's your jersey?

[*She brings the jersey from the bed*]

Here you are. Take your coat off. Get into it.

[*She helps him into his jersey*]

Right. Where's your muffler?

[*She brings a muffler from the bed*]

Here, you are. Wrap it round. That's it. Don't go too fast, Bert, will you? I'll have some cocoa on when you get back. You won't be long. Wait a minute. Where's your overcoat? You'd better put on your overcoat.

[*He fixes his muffler, goes to the door and exits. She stands, watching the door, then turns slowly to the table, picks up the magazine, and puts it down. She stands and listens, goes to the fire, bends, lights the fire and warms her hands. She stands and looks about the room. She looks at the window and listens, goes quickly to the window, stops and straightens the curtain. She comes to the centre of the room, and looks towards the door.*

She goes to the bed, puts on a shawl, goes to the sink, takes a bin from under the sink, goes to the door and opens it]

ROSE: Oh!

[MR *and* MRS SANDS *are disclosed on the landing*]

MRS SANDS: So sorry. We didn't mean to be standing here, like. Didn't mean to give you a fright. We've just come up the stairs.

ROSE: That's all right.

MRS SANDS: This is Mr Sands. I'm Mrs Sands.

ROSE: How do you do?

[MR SANDS *grunts acknowledgement*]

MRS SANDS: We were just going up the stairs. But you can't see a thing in this place. Can you, Toddy?

MR SANDS: Not a thing.

ROSE: What were you looking for?

MRS SANDS: The man who runs the house.

MR SANDS: The landlord. We're trying to get hold of the landlord.

MRS SANDS: What's his name, Toddy?

ROSE: His name's Mr Kidd.

MRS SANDS: Kidd? Was that the name, Toddy?

MR SANDS: Kidd? No, that's not it.

ROSE: Mr Kidd. That's his name.

MR SANDS: Well, that's not the bloke we're looking for.

ROSE: Well, you must be looking for someone else.

[*Pause*]

MR SANDS: I suppose we must be.

ROSE: You look cold.

MRS SANDS: It's murder out. Have you been out?

ROSE: No.

MRS SANDS: We've not long come in.

ROSE: Well, come inside, if you like, and have a warm.

[*They come into the centre of the room*]

[*Bringing the chair from the table to the fire*]   Sit down here. You can get a good warm.

MRS SANDS: Thanks. [*She sits*]

ROSE: Come over by the fire, Mr Sands.

MR SANDS: No, it's all right. I'll just stretch my legs.

MRS SANDS: Why? You haven't been sitting down.

MR SANDS: What about it?

MRS SANDS: Well, why don't you sit down?

MR SANDS: Why should I?

MRS SANDS: You must be cold.

MR SANDS: I'm not.

MRS SANDS: You must be. Bring over a chair and sit down.

MR SANDS: I'm all right standing up, thanks.

MRS SANDS: You don't look one thing or the other standing up.

MR SANDS: I'm quite all right, Clarissa.

ROSE: Clarissa? What a pretty name.

MRS SANDS: Yes, it is nice, isn't it? My father and mother gave it to me.

[*Pause*]

You know, this is a room you can sit down and feel cosy in.

MR SANDS: [*Looking at the room*]   It's a fair size, all right.

MRS SANDS: Why don't you sit down, Mrs—

ROSE: Hudd. No thanks.

MR SANDS: What did you say?

ROSE: When?

MR SANDS: What did you say the name was?

ROSE: Hudd.

MR SANDS: That's it. You're the wife of the bloke you mentioned then?

MRS SANDS: No, she isn't. That was Mr Kidd.

MR SANDS: Was it? I thought it was Hudd.

MRS SANDS: No, it was Kidd. Wasn't it, Mrs Hudd?

ROSE: That's right. The landlord.

MRS SANDS: No, not the landlord. The other man.

ROSE: Well, that's his name. He's the landlord.

MR SANDS: Who?

ROSE: Mr Kidd.

[*Pause*]

MR SANDS: Is he?

MRS SANDS: Maybe there are two landlords.

[*Pause*]

MR SANDS: That'll be the day.

MRS SANDS: What did you say?

MR SANDS: I said that'll be the day.

[*Pause*]

ROSE: What's it like out?

MRS SANDS: It's very dark out.

MR SANDS: No darker than in.

MRS SANDS: He's right there.

MR SANDS: It's darker in than out, for my money.

MRS SANDS: There's not much light in this place, is there, Mrs Hudd? Do you know, this is the first bit of light we've seen since we came in?

MR SANDS: The first crack.

ROSE: I never go out at night. We stay in.

MRS SANDS: Now I come to think of it, I saw a star.

MR SANDS: You saw what?

MRS SANDS: Well, I think I did.

MR SANDS: You think you saw what?

MRS SANDS: A star.

MR SANDS: Where?

MRS SANDS: In the sky.

MR SANDS: When?

MRS SANDS: As we were coming along.

MR SANDS: Go home.

MRS SANDS: What do you mean?

MR SANDS: You didn't see a star.

MRS SANDS: Why not?

MR SANDS: Because I'm telling you. I'm telling you you didn't see a
    star.

    [*Pause*]

ROSE: I hope it's not too dark out. I hope it's not too icy. My
    husband's in his van. He doesn't drive slow either. He never
    drives slow.

MR SANDS: [*Guffawing*]   Well, he's taking a big chance tonight
    then.

ROSE: What?

MR SANDS: No—I mean, it'd be a bit dodgy driving tonight.

ROSE: He's a very good driver.

    [*Pause*]

    How long have you been here?

MRS SANDS: I don't know. How long have we been here, Toddy?

MR SANDS: About half an hour.

MRS SANDS: Longer than that, much longer.

MR SANDS: About thirty-five minutes.

ROSE: Well, I think you'll find Mr Kidd about somewhere. He's
    not long gone to make his tea.

MR SANDS: He lives here, does he?

ROSE: Of course he lives here.

MR SANDS: And you say he's the landlord, is he?

ROSE: Of course he is.

MR SANDS: Well, say I wanted to get hold of him, where would I
    find him?

ROSE: Well—I'm not sure.

MR SANDS: He lives here, does he?

ROSE: Yes, but I don't know—

MR SANDS: You don't know exactly where he hangs out?

ROSE: No, not exactly.

MR SANDS: But he does live here, doesn't he?

  [*Pause*]

MR SANDS: This is a very big house, Toddy.

MR SANDS: Yes, I know it is. But Mrs Hudd seems to know Mr Kidd very well.

ROSE: No, I wouldn't say that. As a matter of fact, I don't know him at all. We're very quiet. We keep ourselves to ourselves. I never interfere. I mean, why should I? We've got our room. We don't bother anyone else. That's the way it should be.

MRS SANDS: It's a nice house, isn't it? Roomy.

ROSE: I don't know about the house. We're all right, but I wouldn't mind betting there's a lot wrong with this house. [*She sits in the rocking chair*] I think there's a lot of damp.

MRS SANDS: Yes, I felt a bit of damp when we were in the basement just now.

ROSE: You were in the basement?

MRS SANDS: Yes, we went down there when we came in.

ROSE: Why?

MRS SANDS: We were looking for the landlord.

ROSE: What was it like down there?

MR SANDS: Couldn't see a thing.

ROSE: Why not?

MR SANDS: There wasn't any light.

ROSE: But what was—you said it was damp?

MRS SANDS: I felt a bit, didn't you, Tod?

MR SANDS: Why? Haven't you ever been down there, Mrs Hudd?

ROSE: Oh yes, once, a long time ago.

MR SANDS: Well, you know what it's like then, don't you?

ROSE: It was a long time ago.

MR SANDS: You haven't been here all that long, have you?

ROSE: I was just wondering whether anyone was living down there now.

MRS SANDS: Yes. A man.

ROSE: A man?

MRS SANDS: Yes.

ROSE: One man?

MR SANDS: Yes, there was a bloke down there, all right.

  [*He perches on the table*]

MRS SANDS: You're sitting down!

MR SANDS: [*jumping up*] Who is?

MRS SANDS: You were.

MR SANDS: Don't be silly. I perched.

MRS SANDS: I saw you sit down.

MR SANDS: You did not see me sit down because I did not sit bloody well down. I perched!

MRS SANDS: Do you think I can't perceive when someone's sitting down?

MR SANDS: Perceive! That's all you do. Perceive.

MRS SANDS: You could do with a bit more of that instead of all that tripe you get up to.

MR SANDS: You don't mind some of that tripe!

MRS SANDS: You take after your uncle, that's who you take after!

MR SANDS: And who do you take after?

MRS SANDS: [*Rising*]   I didn't bring you into the world.

MR SANDS: You didn't what?

MRS SANDS: I said, I didn't bring you into the world.

MR SANDS: Well, who did then? That's what I want to know. Who did? Who did bring me into the world?

[*She sits, muttering. He stands, muttering*]

ROSE: You say you saw a man downstairs, in the basement?

MRS SANDS: Yes, Mrs Hudd, you see, the thing is, Mrs Hudd, we'd heard they'd got a room to let here, so we thought we'd come along and have a look. Because we're looking for a place, you see, somewhere quiet, and we knew this district was quiet, and we passed the house a few months ago and we thought it looked very nice, but we thought we'd call of an evening, to catch the landlord, so we came along this evening. Well, when we got here we walked in the front door and it was very dark in the hall and there wasn't anyone about. So we went down to the basement. Well, we got down there only due to Toddy having such good eyesight really. Between you and me, I didn't like the look of it much, I mean the feel, we couldn't make much out, it smelt damp to me. Anyway, we went through a kind of partition, then there was another partition, and we couldn't see where we were going, well, it seemed to me it got darker the more we went, the further we went in, I thought we must have come to the wrong house. So I stopped. And Toddy stopped. And then this voice said, this voice came—it said—well, it gave me a bit of a fright, I don't know about Tod, but someone asked if he could do anything for us. So Tod said we were looking for the landlord and this man said the landlord would be upstairs. Then Tod asked was there a room vacant. And this man, this voice really, I think he was behind the partition, said yes there was a room vacant. He was very polite, I thought, but we never saw him, I don't know why they never put a light on. Anyway, we got out then and we came up and we went to the top of the house. I don't know whether it was the top. There was a door locked on the stairs, so there might have been another floor, but we didn't see anyone, and it was dark, and we were just coming down again when you opened your door.

ROSE: You said you were going up.

MR SANDS: What?

ROSE: You said you were going up before.

MRS SANDS: No, we were coming down.

ROSE: You didn't say that before.

MRS SANDS: We'd been up.

MR SANDS: We'd been up. We were coming down.

[*Pause*]

ROSE: This man, what was he like, was he old?

MRS SANDS: We didn't see him.

ROSE: Was he old?

[*Pause*]

MR SANDS: Well, we'd better try to get hold of this landlord, if he's about.

ROSE: You won't find any rooms vacant in this house.

MR SANDS: Why not?

ROSE: Mr Kidd told me. He told me.

MR SANDS: Mr Kidd?

ROSE: He told me he was full up.

MR SANDS: The man in the basement said there was one. One room. Number seven he said.

[*Pause*]

ROSE: That's this room.

MR SANDS: We'd better go and get hold of the landlord.

MRS SANDS: [*Rising*] Well, thank you for the warm-up, Mrs Hudd. I feel better now.

ROSE: This room is occupied.

MR SANDS: Come on.

MRS SANDS: Goodnight, Mrs Hudd. I hope your husband won't be too long. Must be lonely for you, being all alone here.

MR SANDS: Come on.

[*They go out.* ROSE *watches the door close, starts towards it, and stops. She takes the chair back to the table, picks up the magazine, looks at it, and puts it down. She goes to the rocking-chair, sits, rocks, stops, and sits still. There is a sharp knock at the door, which opens. Enter* MR KIDD]

MR KIDD: I came straight in.

ROSE: [*Rising*] Mr Kidd! I was just going to find you. I've got to speak to you.

MR KIDD: Look here, Mrs Hudd, I've got to speak to you. I came up specially.

ROSE: There were two people in here just now. They said this room was going vacant. What were they talking about?

MR KIDD: As soon as I heard the van go I got ready to come and see you. I'm knocked out.

ROSE: What was it all about? Did you see those people? How can this room be going? It's occupied. Did they get hold of you, Mr Kidd?

MR KIDD: Get hold of me? Who?

ROSE: I told you. Two people. They were looking for the landlord.

MR KIDD: I'm just telling you. I've been getting ready to come and see you, as soon as I heard the van go.

ROSE: Well then, who were they?

MR KIDD: That's why I came up before. But he hadn't gone yet. I've been waiting for him to go the whole week-end.

ROSE: Mr Kidd, what did they mean about this room?

MR KIDD: What room?

ROSE: Is this room vacant?

MR KIDD: Vacant?

ROSE: They were looking for the landlord.

MR KIDD: Who were?

ROSE: Listen, Mr Kidd, you are the landlord, aren't you? There isn't any other landlord?

MR KIDD: What? What's that got to do with it? I don't know what you're talking about. I've got to tell you, that's all. I've got to tell you. I've had a terrible week-end. You'll have to see him. I can't take it any more. You've got to see him.

[*Pause*]

ROSE: Who?

MR KIDD: The man. He's been waiting to see you. He wants to see you. I can't get rid of him. I'm not a young man, Mrs Hudd, that's apparent. It's apparent. You've got to see him.

ROSE: See who?

MR KIDD: The man. He's downstairs now. He's been there the whole week-end. He said that when Mr Hudd went out I was to tell him. That's why I came up before. But he hadn't gone yet. So I told him. I said he hasn't gone yet. I said, well when he goes, I said, you can go up, go up, have done with it. No, he says, you must ask her if she'll see me. So I came up again, to ask you if you'll see him.

ROSE: Who is he?

MR KIDD: How do I know who he is? All I know is he won't say a word, he won't indulge in any conversation, just—has he gone? that and nothing else. He wouldn't even play a game of chess. All right, I said, the other night, while we're waiting I'll play you a game of chess. You play chess, don't you? I tell you, Mrs Hudd, I don't know if he even heard what I was saying. He just lies there. It's not good for me. He just lies there, that's all, waiting.

ROSE: He lies there, in the basement?

MR KIDD: Shall I tell him it's all right, Mrs Hudd?

ROSE: But it's damp down there.

MR KIDD: Shall I tell him it's all right?

ROSE: That what's all right?

MR KIDD: That you'll see him.

ROSE: See him? I beg your pardon, Mr Kidd. I don't know him. Why should I see him?

MR KIDD: You won't see him?

ROSE: Do you expect me to see someone I don't know? With my husband not here too?

MR KIDD: But he knows you, Mrs Hudd, he knows you.

ROSE: How could he, Mr Kidd, when I don't know him?

MR KIDD: You must know him.

ROSE: But I don't know anybody. We're quiet here. We've just moved into this district.

MR KIDD: But he doesn't come from this district. Perhaps you knew him in another district.

ROSE: Mr Kidd, do you think I go around knowing men in one district after another? What do you think I am?

MR KIDD: I don't know what I think.

[*He sits*]

I think I'm going off my squiff.

ROSE: You need rest. An old man like you. What you need is rest.

MR KIDD: He hasn't given me any rest. Just lying there. In the black dark. Hour after hour. Why don't you leave me be, both of you? Mrs Hudd, have a bit of pity. Please see him. Why don't you see him?

ROSE: I don't know him.

MR KIDD: You can never tell. You might know him.

ROSE: I don't know him.

MR KIDD: [*Rising*]   I don't know what'll happen if you don't see him.

ROSE: I've told you I don't know this man!

MR KIDD: I know what he'll do. I know what he'll do. If you don't see him now, there'll be nothing else for it, he'll come up on his own bat, when your husband's here, that's what he'll do. He'll come up when Mr Hudd's here, when your husband's here.

ROSE: He'd never do that.

MR KIDD: He would do that. That's exactly what he'll do. You don't think he's going to go away without seeing you, after he's come all this way, do you? You don't think that, do you?

ROSE: All this way?

MR KIDD: You don't think he's going to do that, do you?

[*Pause*]

ROSE: He wouldn't do that.

MR KIDD: Oh yes. I know it.

[*Pause*]

ROSE: What's the time?

MR KIDD: I don't know.

[*Pause*]

ROSE: Fetch him. Quick. Quick!

[MR KIDD *goes out. She sits in the rocking-chair*]

[*After a few moments the door opens. Enter a blind Negro. He closes the door behind him, walks further, and feels with a stick till he reaches the armchair. He stops*]

RILEY: Mrs Hudd?

ROSE: You just touched a chair. Why don't you sit in it?

[*He sits*]

RILEY: Thank you.

ROSE: Don't thank me for anything. I don't want you up here. I don't know who you are. And the sooner you get out the better.

[*Pause*]

[*Rising*] Well, come on. Enough's enough. You can take a liberty too far, you know. What do you want? You force your way up here. You disturb my evening. You come in and sit down here. What do you want?

[*He looks about the room*]

What are you looking at? You're blind, aren't you? So what are you looking at? What do you think you've got here, a little girl? I can keep up with you. I'm one ahead of people like you. Tell me what you want and get out.

RILEY: My name is Riley.

ROSE: I don't care if it's—What? That's not your name. That's not your name. You've got a grown-up woman in this room, do you hear? Or are you deaf too? You're not deaf too, are you? You're all deaf and dumb and blind, the lot of you. A bunch of cripples.

[*Pause*]

RILEY: This is a large room.

ROSE: Never mind about the room. What do you know about this room? You know nothing about it. And you won't be staying in it long either. My luck. I get these creeps come in, smelling up my room. What do you want?

RILEY: I want to see you.

ROSE: Well you can't see me, can you? You're a blind man. An old, poor blind man. Aren't you? Can't see a dickeybird.

[*Pause*]

They say I know you. That's an insult, for a start. Because I can tell you, I wouldn't know you to spit on, not from a mile off.

[*Pause*]

Oh, these customers. They come in here and stink the place out. After a handout. I know all about it. And as for you saying you know me, what liberty is that? Telling my landlord too. Upsetting my landlord. What do you think you're up to? We're settled down here, cosy, quiet, and our landlord thinks the world of us, we're his favourite tenants, and you come in and drive him up the wall, and drag my name into it! What did you mean by dragging my name into it, and my husband's name? How did you know what our name was?

[*Pause*]

You've led him a dance, have you, this week-end? You've got him going, have you? A poor, weak old man, who lets a respectable house. Finished. Done for. You push your way in and shove him about. And you drag my name into it.

[*Pause*]

Come on, then. You say you wanted to see me. Well, I'm here. Spit it out or out you go. What do you want?

RILEY: I have a message for you.

ROSE: You've got what? How could you have a message for me, Mister Riley, when I don't know you and nobody knows I'm here and I don't know anybody anyway. You think I'm an easy touch, don't you? Well, why don't you give it up as a bad job? Get off out of it. I've had enough of this. You're not only a nut, you're a blind nut and you can get out the way you came.

[*Pause*]

What message? Who have you got a message from? Who?

RILEY: Your father wants you to come home.

[*Pause*]

ROSE: Home?

RILEY: Yes.

ROSE: Home? Go now. Come on. It's late. It's late.

RILEY: To come home.

ROSE: Stop it. I can't take it. What do you want? What do you want?

RILEY: Come home, Sal.

[*Pause*]

ROSE: What did you call me?

RILEY: Come home, Sal.

ROSE: Don't call me that.

RILEY: Come, now.

ROSE: Don't call me that.

RILEY: So now you're here.

ROSE: Not Sal.

RILEY: Now I touch you.

ROSE: Don't touch me.

RILEY: Sal.

ROSE: I can't.

RILEY: I want you to come home.

ROSE: No.

RILEY: With me.

ROSE: I can't.

RILEY: I waited to see you.

ROSE: Yes.

RILEY: Now I see you.

ROSE: Yes.

RILEY: Sal.

ROSE: Not that.

RILEY: So, now.

[*Pause*]

So, now.

ROSE: I've been here.

RILEY: Yes.

ROSE: Long.

RILEY: Yes.

ROSE: The day is a hump. I never go out.

RILEY: No.

ROSE: I've been here.

RILEY: Come home now, Sal.

[*She touches his eyes, the back of his head and his temples with her hands. Enter* BERT]

[*He stops at the door, then goes to the window and draws the curtains. It is dark. He comes to the centre of the room and regards the woman*]

BERT: I got back all right.

ROSE: [*Going towards him*]   Yes.

BERT: I got back all right.

[*Pause*]

ROSE: Is it late?

BERT: I had a good bowl down there.

[*Pause*]

I drove her down, hard. They got it dark out.

ROSE: Yes.

BERT: Then I drove her back, hard. They got it very icy out.

ROSE: Yes.

BERT: But I drove her.

[*Pause*]

I sped her.

[*Pause*]

I caned her along. She was good. Then I got back. I could see the road all right. There was no cars. One there was. He wouldn't move. I bumped him. I got my road. I had all my way. There again and back. They shoved out of it. I kept on the straight. There was no mixing it. Not with her. She was good. She went with me. She don't mix it with me. I use my hand. Like that. I get hold of her. I go where I go. She took me there. She brought me back.

[*Pause*]

I got back all right.

[*He takes the chair from the table and sits to the left of the* NEGRO'S *chair, close to it. He regards the* NEGRO *for some moments. Then with his foot he lifts the armchair up. The* NEGRO *falls on to the floor. He rises slowly*]

RILEY: Mr Hudd, your wife—

BERT: Lice!

[*He strikes the* NEGRO, *knocking him down, and then kicks his head against the gas stove several times. The* NEGRO *lies still.* BERT *walks away*]

[*Silence*]

[ROSE *stands clutching her eyes*]

ROSE: Can't see. I can't see. I can't see.

Blackout

CURTAIN

PIRANDELLO

The Man with the Flower in his Mouth

All the work of Luigi Pirandello (1867–1936) compassionately examines the anguish of man struggling to come to terms with the enigma of his own personality, and to establish his own identity, both for himself and in relation to others. Pirandello examines again and again the nature of reality, and the sufferings of men faced with uncertainty in regard to it; his most profound concern is always with the subconscious actions and reactions of people, especially those whom life has defeated—the faceless, ordinary people of the crowd. Until they are forced to realise that they will never possess any kind of absolute truth, his characters continually question the nature and purpose of their existence, never abandoning their search for a definite shape in which to cast it. But as each of the illusions behind which they hide from themselves is gradually broken down, they are forced to perceive that ultimately they cannot communicate even with themselves, let alone with others: that they are, in the most final sense, alone. Reality for Pirandello is what we make of it ourselves, so that for each of us it is different. Its only proof is the effect it produces on ourselves and on others.

In exposing for us our secret lives, Pirandello exercises one of the great formative influences on the drama. He extends its frontiers by transforming ideas into living people who engross our intellects as much as they wring our emotions. He gives precise and immediate expression to the abiding problems which beset the lost, the groping, and the truly poor in spirit. He himself defined his purpose thus:

'When someone lives, he lives and does not watch himself. Well, arrange things so that he does watch himself in the act of living, a prey to his passions, by placing a mirror before him; either he will be astonished and dismayed by his own appearance and turn his eyes away so as not to see himself, or he will spit at his image in disgust, or will angrily thrust out his fist to smash it. If he was weeping he will no longer be able to do so, if he was laughing he will no longer be able to laugh. In short, there will be some manifestation of pain. This manifestation of pain is my theatre.'

The Man with the Flower in his Mouth typifies just such a 'manifestation of pain'. The play does not examine a conflict logically from a beginning through a middle to an end. Rather it focuses powerfully and poignantly on the agonising inner struggle of a man trying desperately to come to terms with the inescapable reality of death. In the most succinct and economical way possible, it illustrates the cruellest paradox of human existence of which the experiences of Pirandello's unhappy life had made him aware: that it is only the bitterness of life which forces us to marvel fully at its beauty. As Pirandello wrote to a friend:

'A man, I have tried to tell something to other men, without any ambition, except perhaps that of avenging myself for having been born. And yet life, in spite of all that it has made me suffer, is so beautiful!'

CHARACTERS

THE MAN WITH THE FLOWER IN HIS MOUTH
A PEACEFUL CUSTOMER
Towards the end, at the points indicated, a WOMAN *is seen at the corner, clad in black, and wearing an old hat with drooping feathers.*

The Man with the Flower in his Mouth

Scene: At the back, we see the trees of an avenue and electric lights showing through the leaves. On both sides, the last houses of a street which leads into this avenue. Among the houses on the left, a cheap all-night café, with chairs and little tables on the sidewalk. In front of the houses on the right, a streetlamp, lit. On the left, where the street meets the avenue, there is another lamp affixed to the corner house; it too is lit. At intervals, the vibrant notes of a mandolin are heard in the distance.

When the curtain rises, THE MAN WITH THE FLOWER IN HIS MOUTH *is sitting at a table and looking in silence at the* PEACEFUL CUSTOMER *who is at the next table, sucking a mint frappé through a straw.*

MAN: Well, what I was just going to say . . . Here you are, a law-abiding sort of man . . . You missed your train?

CUSTOMER: By one minute. I get to the station and see the damn thing just pulling out.

MAN: You could have run after it.

CUSTOMER: Sure—but for those damn packages. I looked like an old packhorse covered with luggage. Isn't that silly? But you know how women are. Errands, errands, errands! You're never through. God! You know how long it took me to get my fingers on the strings of all those packages—when I climbed out of the cab? Three solid minutes. Two packages to each finger.

MAN: What a sight! Know what *I'd* have done? Left 'em in the cab.

CUSTOMER: How about my wife? And my daughters? And all the other women?

MAN: They'd squawk. I'd enjoy that.

CUSTOMER: You don't seem to know how women carry on when they get out in the country.

MAN: I know exactly how they carry on. [*Pause*] They tell you they won't need a thing, they can live on nothing.

CUSTOMER: Worse, they pretend they live there to *save* money. They go out to one of those villages*—the uglier and filthier the better—and then insist on wearing all their fanciest get-ups! Women! But I suppose it's their vocation. 'If you're going into town, could you get me one of these—and one of those—and

---

* The scene is rather obviously laid in Rome. The villages where 'commuters' live are some ten miles out. [E.B.]

would it trouble you *too* much to get me . . .' Would it trouble you *too* much! 'And since you'll be right next door to . . .' 'Now really, darling, how do you expect me to get all that done in three hours?' 'Why not? Can't you take a cab?' And the hell of it is—figuring on those three hours—I didn't bring the keys to our house here in town.

MAN: Quite a thing. So?

CUSTOMER: I left my pile of packages at the station—in the parcel room. Then I went to a restaurant for supper. Then I went to the theatre—to get rid of my bad temper. The heat nearly killed me. Coming out, I say: 'And now, what? It's after midnight. There isn't a train till four. All that fuss for a couple of hours of sleep? Not worth the price of the ticket.' So here I am. Open all night, isn't it?

MAN: All night. [*Pause*]   So you left your packages in the parcel room?

CUSTOMER: Why do you ask? Don't you think they're safe? They were tied up good and . . .

MAN: Oh, sure, sure! [*Pause*]   I feel *sure* they're safe. I know how well these salesmen wrap their stuff. They make quite a speciality of it. [*Pause*]   I can see their hands now. What hands! They take a good big piece of paper, double thickness, sort of a reddish colour, wavy lines on it—a pleasure just to look at it!—so smooth, you could press it against your cheek and feel how cool and delicate it is . . . They roll it out on the counter and then place your cloth in the middle of it with *such* agility—fine cloth too, neatly folded. They raise one edge of the paper with the back of the hand, lower the other one, and bring the two edges together in an elegant fold—*that's* just thrown in for good measure . . . Then they fold the corners down in a triangle with its apex turned in like this. Then they reach out with one hand for the box of string, instinctively pull off just exactly enough, and tie up the parcel so quickly you haven't even time to admire their . . . virtuosity—the little loop is ready for your finger!

CUSTOMER: Anyone can see you've given a lot of attention to this matter.

MAN: Have I! My dear man, I spend whole days at it. What's more, I can spend a solid hour at a single store window. I lose myself in it. I seem to *be* that piece of silk, I'd *like* to be that piece of silk, that bit of braid, that ribbon—red or blue—that the salesgirls are measuring with their tape and—you've seen what they do with it before they wrap it up?—they twist it round the thumb and little finger of their left hand in a figure eight! [*Pause*]   I look at the shoppers as they come out of the store with their bundle on their finger—or in their hand—or under their arm. I watch them pass. My eyes follow them till they're out of sight. I imagine, oh, I imagine so many, many things, you've no idea, how could you have? [*Pause. Then, darkly, as to himself*]   All the same, it helps.

CUSTOMER: What helps?

MAN: Latching on—to life. With the imagination. Like a creeper around the bars of a gate. [*Pause*]   Giving it no rest—my imagination, I mean—clinging, clinging with my imagination to the lives of others—all the time. Not people I know, of course. I couldn't do that. That'd be annoying, it'd nauseate me if *they* knew. No. Just strangers. With them my imagination can work freely. Not capriciously, though. Oh no, I take account of the smallest things I can find out about them. You've no idea how my imagination functions. I work my way *in*. In! I get to see this man's house—or that man's, I live in it, I feel I belong there. And I begin to notice—you know how a house, any old house, has its own air, how there's something special about the air in it? Your house? Mine? Of course, in your own house, you don't notice it any more, it's *your* air, the air of *your* life, isn't it? Uh huh. I see you agree—

CUSTOMER: I only meant . . . well, I was thinking what a good time you must have imagining all this!

MAN: [*Annoyed, after thinking a moment*]   Good time? I had a——!

CUSTOMER: Good time, yes. I can just see you——

MAN: Tell me something. Did you ever consult an eminent physician?

CUSTOMER: Me? Why should I? I'm not sick!

MAN: Just a moment. I ask because I'd like to know if you ever saw a fine doctor's waiting room—full of patients waiting their turn?

CUSTOMER: Well, yes. I once had to take my little girl. She's nervous.

MAN: Okay. You needn't tell me. It's the waiting rooms . . . [*Pause*]   Have you ever given them much attention? The old-fashioned couch with dark covers, the upholstered table chairs that don't match as a rule . . . the armchairs? Stuff bought at sales and auctions, coming together there by accident, for the convenience of the patients. It doesn't belong to the house. The doctor has quite another sort of room for himself, for his wife, his wife's friends . . . lavish . . . lovely . . . If you took one of the chairs from the drawing room and put it in the waiting room, why, it'd stick out like a sore thumb. Not that the waiting room isn't just right—nothing special of course but quite proper, quite respectable . . . I'd like to know if you—when you went with your little girl—if you took a good look at the chair you sat in?

CUSTOMER:: Well, um, no, I guess I didn't.

MAN: Of course not. You weren't sick . . . [*Pause*] But often even the sick don't notice. They're all taken up with their sickness. [*Pause*] How many times they sit, some of them, staring at their finger which is making meaningless markings on the polished arm of the chair. They're thinking—so they don't see. [*Pause*] And what an impression you get when you get out of the doctor's office and cross the waiting room and see the chair you'd been sitting in awaiting sentence on the as yet unknown sickness just a short time before! Now, there's another patient on it and *he's* hugging his secret sickness too. Or it's empty—oh, how *impassive* it looks!—waiting for Mr X to come and sit on it. [*Pause*] What were we saying? Oh, yes. The pleasure of imagining things. And I suddenly thought of a chair in one of those waiting rooms. Why?

CUSTOMER: Yes, it certainly . . .

MAN: You don't see the connection? Neither do I. [*Pause*] You recall an image, you recall another image, they're unrelated, and yet—they're *not* unrelated—for you. Oh, no, they have their reasons, they stem from *your* experience. Of course you have to pretend they don't. When you talk, you have to forget them. Most often they're so illogical, these . . . analogies. [*Pause*] The connection could be this, maybe. Listen. Do you think those chairs get any pleasure from imagining which patient will sit on them next? What sickness lurks inside him? Where he'll go, what he'll do after this visit? Of course they don't. And it's the same with me! I get no pleasure from it. There are those poor chairs and here am I. *They* open their arms to the doctor's patients, I open mine to . . . this person or that. You for instance. And yet I get no pleasure—no pleasure at all—from the train you missed, the family waiting for that train in the country, your other little troubles . . .

CUSTOMER: I've plenty, you know that?

MAN: You should thank God they're little. [*Pause*] Some people have big troubles, my dear sir. [*Pause*] As I was saying, I feel the need to latch on—by the skin of my . . . imagination—to the lives of others. Yet I get no pleasure from this. It doesn't even interest me. Quite the reverse, quite . . . One wants to see what their troubles are just to prove to oneself that life is idiotic and stupid! So that one won't mind being through with it!! [*With dark rage*] Proving that to yourself takes quite a bit of doing, huh? You need evidence, you need a hundred and one instances, and—you—must—be—*implacable!* Because, well, because, my dear sir, there's something—we don't know what it's made of, but it exists—and we all feel it, we feel it like a pain in the throat—it's the hunger for life! A hunger that is never appeased—that never *can* be appeased—because life—life as we live it from moment to moment—is so hungry itself, hungry *for* itself, we never get to taste it even! The taste of life, the flavour and savour of life, is all in the past, we carry it inside us. Or rather it's always at a distance from us. We're tied to it only by a slender thread, the rope of memory. Yes, memory ties us to . . . what? that idiocy, these irritations, those silly illusions, mad pursuits like . . . yes . . . What today is idiocy, what today is an irritation, even what today is a misfortune, a grave misfortune, look! Four years pass, five years, ten, and who knows what savour or flavour it will have, what tears will be shed over it, how—it—will—*taste!* Life, life! You only have to think of giving it up—especially if it's a matter of days—[*At this point the head of* THE WOMAN IN BLACK *is seen at the corner*] Look! See that? At the corner! See that woman, that shadow of a woman? She's hiding now.

CUSTOMER: What? Who was it?

MAN: You didn't see? She's hiding now.

CUSTOMER: A woman?

MAN: My wife.

CUSTOMER: Ah! Your wife? [*Pause*]

MAN: She keeps an eye on me. Oh, sometimes I could just go over and kick her! It wouldn't do any good, though. She's as stubborn as a lost dog: the more you kick it, the closer it sticks to you. [*Pause*] What that woman is suffering on my account you could not imagine. She doesn't eat. Doesn't sleep any more. Just follows me around. Night and day. At a distance. She *might* brush her clothes once in a while—and that old shoe of a hat. She isn't a woman any more. Just—a rag doll. Her hair's going grey, yes, the white dust has settled on her temples forever, and she's only thirty-four. [*Pause*] She annoys me. You wouldn't believe how much she annoys me. Sometimes I grab hold of her and shake her. 'You're an idiot!' I shout. She takes it. She stands there looking at me. Oh, that look! It makes my fingers itch. I feel like strangling her! Nothing happens, of course. She just waits till I'm a short way off. Then she starts following me again. [THE WOMAN IN BLACK *again sticks her head out*]   Look! There's her head again!

CUSTOMER: Poor woman!

MAN: Poor woman? You know what she wants? She wants me to stay and take it easy at home—all cosy and quiet—and let her be nice to me, look after me, show me wifely tenderness . . . Home! The rooms in perfect order, the furniture elegant and neat, silence reigns . . . It used to, anyway. Silence—measured by the tick-tocking of the dining-room clock! [*Pause*]   That's what she wants! I just want you to see the absurdity of it! Isn't it absurd? It's worse: it's cruel, it's macabre! Don't you see? Think of Messina. Or Avezzano. Suppose they knew an earthquake was coming. Do you think those cities could just sit? You think they could just sit calmly in the moonlight waiting for it? Carefully preserving the lovely lines of their streets and the spaciousness of their piazzas? Not daring to deviate one inch from the plans of the City Planning Commission? You're crazy. Those cities would drop everything and take to their heels! Every house, every stone, would take to its heels! [*Wheeling on the* CUSTOMER]   You agree?

CUSTOMER: [*Frightened*] Well . . .

MAN: Well, just suppose the people knew? The citizens of Avezzano and Messina. Would they calmly get undressed and go to bed? Fold their clothes and put their shoes outside the door? Creep down under the bedclothes and enjoy the nice clean feeling of freshly laundered sheets? Knowing that—in a few hours—they would be dead?—You think they might?

CUSTOMER: Maybe your wife——

MAN: Let me finish. [*Starting over*]   If death, my dear sir, if death were some strange, filthy insect that just . . . settled on you, as it were, took you unawares, shall we say . . . You're walking along. All of a sudden a passerby stops you, and, with finger and thumb cautiously extended, says: 'Excuse me, sir, excuse me, honoured sir, but death has settled on you!' And with finger and thumb cautiously extended, he takes it and throws it in the gutter. Wouldn't that be wonderful? But death is not an insect. It has settled on many walkers in the city—however far away their thoughts may be, however carefree they may feel. They don't see it. They're thinking what they'll be doing tomorrow. But I [*He gets up*]   . . . Look, my dear sir, come here [*He gets the* CUSTOMER *up and takes him under the lighted lamp*] under the lamp. Come over here. I'll show you something. Look! Under this side of my moustache. See that little knob? Royal purple? Know what they call it? It has such a poetic name. It suggests something soft and sweet. Like a caramel. Epithelioma. [*The 'o' is stressed*]   Try it, isn't it soft and sweet? Epithelioma. Understand? Death passed my way. He stuck this . . . flower in my mouth and said: 'Keep it, old chap. I'll stop by again in eight months—or maybe ten.' [*Pause*]   Now tell me. *You* tell *me*. Can I just sit quietly at home as that unhappy girl wishes me to—with this flower in my mouth? [*Pause*]   I yell at her. 'So you want me to kiss you, do you?' 'Yes, yes, kiss me!' You know what she did? A couple of weeks ago she took a pin and cut herself—here—on the lip—then she took hold of my head and tried to kiss me, tried to kiss me on the mouth. She said she wanted to die with me. [*Pause*]   She's insane. [*Angrily*]   I'm not home! Ever! What I want is to stand at store windows admiring the virtuosity of salesmen! Because, you see, if ever, for one second, I am not occupied, if ever I'm *empty*—know what I mean?—why, I might take a life and think nothing of it, I might destroy the life in someone . . . someone I don't even know, I'd take a gun and kill someone—like you maybe—someone who's missed his train. [*He laughs*]   Of course, I'm only joking. [*Pause*]   I'll go now. [*Pause*]   It'd be myself I'd kill. [*Pause*]   At this time of year, there's a certain kind of apricot, it's good . . . How do *you* eat them? Skin and all? You cut them in exact halves, you take hold with finger and thumb, lengthwise, like this . . . then! [*He swallows*]   How succulent! Pure delight! Like a woman's lips! [*He laughs. Pause*]   I wish to send my best wishes to your good lady and her daughters in your country home. [*Pause*]   I imagine them . . . I imagine them dressed in white and light blue in the middle of a lovely green meadow under the shade of . . . [*Pause*]   Will you do me a favour when you arrive, tomorrow morning? As I figure it, your village is a certain distance from the station. It is dawn. You will be on foot. The first tuft of grass you see by the roadside—count the number of blades, will you? Just count the blades of grass. The number will be the number of days I have to live. [*Pause*]   One last request: pick a big tuft! [*He laughs*]   Then: Good night!

He walks away humming through closed lips the tune which the mandolin is playing in the distance. He is approaching the corner on the right. But at a certain point—remembering his Wife—he turns and sneaks off in the opposite direction. The CUSTOMER *follows with his eyes—more or less dumb-founded*]

CURTAIN

Points for Discussion

A Wedding

1. Examine the behaviour of the characters in the play. Each persists in behaving rigidly and uncompromisingly. How is this fact responsible for both the action and the humour of the play?

2. Compare the play's beginning with its ending. How are these similar? Has there been any progression or development in the characters or their motivations during the course of the play?

3. The situation of the play appears to be quite normal on the surface. Is it so in reality?

4. Suggest some of the events which might take place after the final curtain has fallen. Is there any real possibility of a resolution to the situation after we have left it?

5. To judge from the structure of this play alone, how would you define 'farce'?

6. How in this play do you think Chekhov manages to 'say honestly to people: "Have a look at yourselves and see how bad and dreary your lives are"'?

7. Where does the play become more pathetic than ridiculous? Why is this?

8. The play is set in Tsarist Russia, and the main event of its plot derives from the snob values of this old regime. Do you think this makes the play an outmoded 'period piece' or not?

This Property is Condemned

1. In what way does the visual appearance of Willie define her character and her motivations? How is it simultaneously ridiculous and pathetic?

2. What dramatic purpose is served by Willie's 'crazy doll'? Is it merely a child's property, or does it have a deeper significance in the context of the play as a whole?

3. What is the significance of the repeated references to 'the sky, white as a clean piece of paper'?

4. Define the roles in the play of the boy Tom and the unseen Frank Waters. How do they counterpoint each other? Why are they both necessary to the play's dramatic purpose?

5. Explain the dramatic irony in Willie's frequent reference to Greta Garbo in *Camille*, and to Alva's favourite song, 'You're the only star in my blue heaven'. In what way do these references define the play's purpose?

6. Though Alva is dead, she is the play's chief character. Discuss how and why she is so.

7. Comment on the significance of the play's title. How is it given heightened dramatic significance by the setting of the play's action near a derelict house on a railway embankment?

The Two Executioners

1. Motivate all Françoise's actions as fully as possible. Comment on the difference between what she does, and what she *says* she does.

2. 'How good you are, mother, how good you are!' Benoît keeps repeating. In what sense is she 'good'? Is she 'good' in any absolute sense?

3. Françoise repeatedly justifies her conduct by invoking religious values in religious imagery. In what sense are these values true? How does Françoise invalidate them?

4. Purgation through suffering is an old theological ideal. It is used by Françoise to console her husband in his suffering. Is it really consolation? Does the ideal remain valid in this situation?

5. Define the physical and symbolic role of the Two Executioners.

6. Of what crimes do you think Jean is guilty? Is it in any way true to say that he is in fact responsible for his own death, as Françoise says?

7. Why is Maurice 'unnatural as ever' in his mother's eyes? Is he really 'unnatural'? What dilemma does he face?

8. Why does Arrabal confront two *boys* with this dilemma, rather than two men? In what way do they thus become more symbolic of all mankind?

9. Why is the ending of the play not an affirmation but a total negation of the traditional values invoked throughout?

The End of the Beginning

1. Describe Darry's character in detail as it is revealed through his relationship with his wife and his friend.

2. Darry is constantly seeking status in the eyes of his wife, his friend, and society at large. How does he set about getting it? Why do his efforts only succeed in making him ridiculous?

3. In what way does the song the two men rehearse have a direct bearing on the theme of the play?

4. Discuss the play's dramatic technique. How does O'Casey progressively build up both the play's humour and its tension?

5. Comment on the effectiveness of the play's last line and its value in summing up the problem posed in the play.

6. Explain the aptness of the play's title.

7. Is this a comedy or a farce? What is the difference?

The Trojan Women

1. Examine the roles played by the gods throughout the play. In what way are they, in Sartre's words, 'powerful and ridiculous at the same time'?

2. How does the fact that the gods are capricious and unreasonable increase the suffering and tragedy of the mortals?

3. Examine Hecuba's first great lament. Is there any evidence to agree with Sartre, who pointed to 'the ambivalent attitude of Hecuba herself who, at times, is content to abandon Troy to its misfortune, while at others she rails against the injustice which has caused it'. If her attitude is ambivalent, what is the cause of it? How does it increase her own tragedy and the tragic irony of the play as a whole?

4. What is your reaction to the character of Talthybios? What dramatic purpose does he serve? How does he increase the play's tragic tension?

5. Define the tragedy of Cassandra. How does it differ from the tragedy of the other women? Is it greater or less?

6. How does Sartre dramatise his censure of 'the sudden switch of that little bourgeoise, Andromeda, who first produces all the attitudes of a wife, then switches to those of a mother'. Do you think, in terms of the problem which the play is presenting, that Andromeda deserves this censure?

7. Throughout the play, the men blame the gods, and the gods, at the end, blame the men. Who must ultimately bear the responsibility? Why?

The Room

1. Examine Rose's opening speech. What does it tell you about the kind of woman she is? What key ideas are continually repeated? Why does Rose repeat them so often?
2. How does Rose treat Bert? How does he treat her? What light does this shed on their relationship?
3. Why does Rose want to keep Bert in the room and not let him go out? What is her attitude to the rest of the house? How is it synonymous with her attitude to the outside world?
4. Discuss how the sense of vagueness, uncertainty and suspense is built up throughout the play. How does the door play a vital role in this build-up?
5. See how many times (a) Mr Kidd; (b) Mr and Mrs Sands refuse to answer questions directly put to them. What does this evasion (or unawareness) reveal about them in each case?
6. Examine all the references in the play to light and darkness. Are they all meant to be taken literally, or do they assume a metaphorical or symbolic significance?
7. How are light and darkness related to the blindness of the Negro and, at the end, to that of Rose?
8. How do the events of the play illustrate Pinter's belief that 'there are no hard distinctions between what is real and what is unreal, nor between what is true and what is false'?

The Man with the Flower in his Mouth

1. Why does the dramatist refuse to name the characters of this play? How are their natures defined simply by his description of them as 'the man with the flower in his mouth' and 'a peaceful customer'?
2. Why does the man persist in 'clinging with (his) imagination to the lives of others . . . like a creeper around the bars of a gate'? How does he do this?
3. Examine his descriptions of (a) salesmen making up parcels; (b) a doctor's waiting-room. What makes these descriptions vivid? How do they define the man's suffering? Do you find them moving?
4. Discuss the relationship between the man and his wife. Why does she persist in following him? Does she achieve her purpose?
5. Show how in this play Pirandello illustrates his belief that reality is what we make of it ourselves.